# OLD GLASS

## EUROPEAN AND AMERICAN

"Decanters, Rummers, Drams and Masons,
Flutes, Hob-nobs, Crofts and Finger Baisins
Proof Bottles, Goblets, Cans and Wines,
Punch Juggs, Liqueurs and Gardevines,
Salts, Mustards, Salads, Butter Keelers,
And all that's sold by other dealers.
Engraved or cut in newest taste,
Or plain, whichever pleases best."

*Cork New Evening Post.* 1792.

STIEGEL CUP, BUSWELL COLLECTION

*(Frontispiece)*

# OLD GLASS

## EUROPEAN AND AMERICAN

BY

## N. HUDSON MOORE

AUTHOR OF

"THE OLD CLOCK BOOK," "THE OLD CHINA BOOK,"
"THE OLD FURNITURE BOOK," "OLD PEWTER,
BRASS, COPPER AND SHEFFIELD PLATE,"
"THE OLD LACE BOOK," ETC.

*WITH TWO HUNDRED AND SIXTY-FIVE*
*ILLUSTRATIONS*

TUDOR  PUBLISHING  CO.
NEW YORK

TUDOR PUBLISHING CO. 1946.
*Copyright, 1924, by*
FREDERICK A. STOKES COMPANY

PRINTED IN THE UNITED STATES OF AMERICA
*By Montauk Book Manufacturing Co., Inc., New York*

# CONTENTS

## PART I

## PART II

# CONTENTS

# LIST OF ILLUSTRATIONS

# ILLUSTRATIONS

# ILLUSTRATIONS

# ILLUSTRATIONS

# ILLUSTRATIONS

# ILLUSTRATIONS

# ILLUSTRATIONS

# ILLUSTRATIONS

# ILLUSTRATIONS

# ILLUSTRATIONS

# PART I

# OLD GLASS

## THE ART OF GLASS-MAKING

ALTHOUGH this book deals with Old Glass, I am not going back to Tubal Cain. Nor am I about to quote what Pliny, the Roman historian (A.D. 23 to 79), wrote about its discovery, for there are other historians who think he was mistaken, since it is impossible to make glass in the open air and under the conditions he describes.

But it is a known fact that the Egyptians were early in the field as glass-makers of skill and that the Romans copied their product. At the Metropolitan Museum in New York, in the Edward C. Moore collection, are some beautiful examples of small, coloured, moulded Roman glass vases. These vases are said to date back to the first century B.C. This period is given by some authorities as the date of the invention of the blowpipe. From this time till the fifth century, this method— blowing in a mould—was in constant use among the Roman glass-blowers and the making of glass had become a highly developed art.

In fact the Romans used glass for more domestic purposes than it is used at the present day, for having no highly glazed or fine porcelain, glass objects, both coloured and plain, took their place for household use. It is seldom remembered that the Portland or Barberini vase in the British Museum, London, which Wedgwood so successfully copied, is of glass, cameo glass it was called. This was made by putting successive layers of glass over the original gathering, and then cutting away the outer coat from the portion which was to form the background, leaving the decoration white or whatever colour was selected.

The Barberini vase was found in the sixteenth century in a sarcophagus near Rome. It belonged to the Barberini family for nearly two centuries and then was bought by the Duchess of Portland and lent to the British Museum, where it is still to be seen. This vase is supposed to have been made in the time of Antoninus, that is, 138-161 A.D. In addition to resisting the corroding tooth of time, this vase, smashed into many pieces by a stick in the hands of a lunatic, has emerged again triumphant. It has been restored so successfully that it is hardly possible to detect the places where it has been joined.

Constantine the Great (*b.* 288, *d.* 337 A.D.) and Theodosius II (*b.* 401, *d.* 450 A.D.) encouraged glassmaking in the East and urged skilled workmen to come to the seat of their empire, and the making of glass flourished greatly. There still remain some of these beautiful glass objects, particularly of Greek and Roman manufacture, to prove the versatility of the artists who made them. Two which are owned by the Victoria and Albert Museum, London, are shown here.

Figure 1 is described as a bottle of glass, "Alabastos," with broad lip and two small ears; green, with yellow and white wavy lines; from a Greek tomb, probably of the fifth century B.C. The second vase, Figure 2, is quite as beautiful, and may have been from its small size and shape used for some toilet article, holding perfume, ointment or some rare drug. It is three and a half inches tall, and could have been conveniently carried on the person. The colour is blue, and the decorations are in turquoise blue and yellow. This was also from a Greek tomb, probably of the fifth century B.C.

It was not till the fifth century A.D. that the Western world began to challenge the supremacy of the East, and the Venetian Republic became the leader in the manufacture of glass. The Venetians were clever, they sought to prevent the trade secrets of glass-making from becoming known. So about the end of the thirteenth century they confined their workmen to the Island of Murano, which is separated from Venice by a narrow strip of water. They traded with countries in the Far East and Venice became wealthy through her glass trade.

In this same century and in the fourteenth and fifteenth the Saracens made very choice glass. Dillon in "Glass" speaks particularly of the beauty of the enam-

*Figures 1 and 2, page 15.*

elled pieces, and says that even yet occasional pieces are found in England and France. This enamelled glass was made in lamps, vases, beakers, and bottles, particularly for mosques. It is seldom that a piece finds its way to America.

Figure 3 shows a vase in the Victoria and Albert Museum, London. It is 17½ inches tall, of clear glass painted in enamel colours, chiefly blue and red and gold. Round the body is an Arabic inscription in Neshky characters, "Glory to our Lord the Sultan, the wise, just, religious warrior, king." The first part of this is repeated around the neck. From Cairo, of the fourteenth century.

About this period the Germans began to manufacture glass, but their product was coarse and heavy, decorated with enamels and entirely lacking the grace and beauty of the Venetian output. Assyria, India, China, Persia, Spain as well as Egypt made glass with more or less success, and at different periods. Italy, Germany, the Low Countries, France and England were the leaders and remain so still, although America is not far behind.

For centuries the Venetian models were copied everywhere. Even Persia used their designs, often used decoration of gold, and to-day the modern Persian glass differs very little from the Venetian glass of the sixteenth and seventeenth centuries. Figure 4 shows some typical pieces which are in the Pennsylvania Mu-

*Figures 3 and 4, pages 16 and 17.*

seum, Philadelphia. They belong to the eighteenth century.

Excelling in all branches of the ceramic art, China does not seem to have given the same amount of attention to the making of glass. It was mentioned by a Chinese writer in 627 A.D., but little is known of the manufacture before the eighteenth century. Figure 5 shows one vase of a pair in dark blue glass, in the Victoria and Albert Museum, London. It is engraved in relief with an Arabic inscription, and also with the seal of Yung-cheng, A.D. 1723-35.

Figure 6, a vase of sapphire glass, has on it the seal mark of Ch'ien-lung, A.D. 1736-95. The Chinese are making to-day glass of extreme beauty of colour and of graceful shapes, flat bowls, vases, small dishes. The colours are greens, blues, soft yellow and a glowing ruby, all of them translucent and showing to wonderful advantage against the light. Under the heading of glass may come those entrancing objects used by the Chinese for medicine, snuff or perfume. Sometimes they are made of clear glass and exquisitely painted on the inside with landscapes, birds, fishes, anything which appeals to their delicate fancy. Other bottles are cut from blocks of glass, coloured quartz or crystal, and they make one of the most charming as well as costly bibelots which one can collect. For years I have had it in my mind that I would own some of these pretty things, but since a collector of old American glass, who

*Figures 5 and 6, page 18.*

does not hesitate to pay hundreds of dollars for choice specimens, advised me to "forget it," that ruin lay in the path of the collector of really choice snuff bottles, why, I have tried to follow his advice, and so far I have only two.

Another object which appeals to the collector is the ruby shade of Bohemian glass. This they succeeded in making during the early part of the seventeenth century. But before they attempted colour they excelled in making a superior clear glass. In 1609, Caspar Lehmann, a Bohemian glass-worker, invented the process of engraving on glass, which gave a new impulse to the industry. The distribution of glass was more general and its uses more various than one is apt to realise, even at this early period. Craddock, an Englishman, writing about 1650, mentions that blown glass, "black and strong," was used in making the black-and-white pavements which were so popular. Tournefort, the distinguished French botanist who travelled so extensively in the East, mentions in 1683 that "in the palace at Teflis there were windows glazed with great squares of blue, yellow, grey, and other coloured glasses."

England, curiously enough, seemed content to get her rich glass from Venice, in cups, flagons and bottles, and not try herself to build up the industry. But during the reign of Elizabeth, she appreciated the value of glass-works and invited to London a glass-worker named Cornelius De Lannoy; he established glasshouses and from this time on the British Isles had an important part in the industry.

Even before this time there had been a little glass made in England, but the introduction of flint glass was an important step forward. It was made first by the Venetians from crystal pebbles which they got from their rivers, and ground. When the first Venetian glassmakers came to England they used the native flints for their glass, and even after silicious sand was used, the name flint glass still clung. The old formula for flint glass was sand, lead, potash, salpetre and manganese. Common glass for bottle-making contained sand, soaper's waste, gas lime, common clay and rock salt.*

This latter formula produced a glass which was green in colour, known as bottle glass, but when carefully made and rendered colourless by the use of manganese, it was called crown glass. Apsley Pellatt in his "Curiosities of Glass Making," published in 1849, gives many formulas for the making of coloured glass:

For blue transparent glass, oxide of cobalt was added to the formula already given for flint glass.

For ruby red, oxide of gold was added.

For amethyst or purple, add oxide of manganese.

For emerald green, add copper scales and iron ore.

For common orange, there was added iron and manganese.

* Apsley Pellatt: "Curiosities of Glass Making."

For gold topaz, add oxide of uranium.

For soft white opaque enamel, add arsenic and antimony.

For hard white opaque enamel, add putty prepared from tin and lead.

In all batches of material for making glass, either common, green, or flint, it was found that the "metal," as the molten glass was called, had a much better quality if there was added broken glass, even sometimes as much as one-quarter in bulk. This was called "cullet," and was constantly called for in advertisements, in both English and early American newspapers.

The flint glass of to-day is probably very different from that made in the sixteenth and seventeenth centuries. The term is now understood to mean a glass composed of silicates of potash and lead. It is the most brilliant and colourless of all glasses, and England claims that she was the first to perfect it. Hartshorne in "Old English Glasses" dates its discovery about 1663, when a patent for making "crystal glass" was taken out by a man named Tilson. On the other hand, E. W. Hulme, who spent years investigating the subject, and who wrote "English Glass Making in the XVI and XVII Centuries," gives the date as 1730, when flint glass in its present form was perfected.

One of the chief beauties of ancient glass is its pleasing irregularity. There is a freedom in the decoration, often crookedness in the whole object which was the result of hand work. A most important thing in the manufacture of glass was the building of the pots in which it was made. These were subjected to such intense heat that the process of making them was a difficult one. If not made of the best materials they would crack, in which case the metal would be lost. Old pots broken up and ground down, then mixed with new clay were found to give the best results, the proportion being about one to three. These pots were built up layer upon layer, each successive layer being carefully dried, so that the process was a lengthy one, and from six months to a year was not an undue time to give to the making.

The earliest glass was made in open pots with wood as a fuel. In order to obtain an abundance of fuel the glass-works were situated in the country. In the year 1641, a bill was introduced in England to stop the felling of trees for burning glass, and from the last quarter of the seventeenth century, glass-works were in or near towns where coal could be obtained. With the use of coal, gases arose which were injurious to the molten metal, so it was found necessary to cover the pots.

The number of pots which glass-houses employed varied. Dudley Westropp, in his book on "Irish Glass," gives as follows the method of working a ten-pot furnace:

"Each glass-blower had a chair with long arms on which he rotated the blowing-iron with the gathering of glass. The four or five chair system was the one usually employed. For a ten-pot furnace four or five sets of workmen would be employed in making the glass objects while the other four or five rested. The first chair was termed the castor hole chair, consisting of a blower and three assistants, known as servitor, footmaker, and taker-in or boy, and was used for large pieces, jugs, decanters, etc. This chair had an empty pot heated with dried beechwood, for reheating the glass.

"The second chair, consisting of four workmen, made fancy articles, goods required for cutting, chemical apparatus, etc. This chair reheated the glass at the mouth of one of the pots containing fluid metal. The third chair, also consisting of four workmen, made almost exclusively wine glasses, goblets, tumblers, lamp chimneys, etc. The fourth chair, consisting of four or five workmen, did not require such skilled operators as the other three, and made chiefly phials and small articles."

The tools used by glass-makers have varied little in several centuries. A list of tools published in "The Toast," 1747, reads, "bars, paddles, rakes, ladles, pipes, pontee stakes, shears, scissors, crannies and towers." Hunter, in "Stiegei Glass," gives as the tools employed, blow-pipe, pucellas, which are a pair of shears looking something like garden shears, and used for everything but cutting, the blades being dull. There are also short-bladed shears, tongs for picking up small objects, a trowel-like tool with a handle, used for shaping, and finally the pontil or punty.

In addition to the glass-maker's chair with arms, he also uses a stout table with an iron top, called a marver, on which he rolls into shape the small bunch of glass, called the "gathering," which he has attached to the blow-pipe.

In "Glass Making in All Ages," Walter Rosenhain says: "Large objects like carboys were difficult to blow on account of the weight of glass to be handled by the gatherer and blower. In the old days the only aid available to the blower was the method of injecting into the partially blown carboy a small quantity of either water or alcohol. This liquid was vaporized immediately by the heat of the glass, and if the blower held his thumb over the opening in the blowpipe, the force of the vapor blew out the glass to the proper extent."

The cooling of glass objects is almost as important as blowing them. For too sudden chilling renders them liable to break. They are gradually cooled by placing them in an annealing oven which is allowed to grow cool slowly, or by slowly removing the glass from a constant source of heat.

It requires considerable skill to coil the proper amount of glass on an iron rod four feet long. This mass of glass is slightly rolled on the marver to solidify it, and then somewhat hollowed by blowing.

The moulds were used to give shape to the vessels,

and also to impress patterns upon them. They were formerly made of wood or iron.

The operation of cutting glass from the brilliant lead glass blanks is now purely mechanical. The old and new methods are contrasted in "The Journal of Industrial and Engineering Chemistry." "Patterns were marked out on the blank, and steel wheels, with mitred edges and armed with trickling sand and water, were used to make the deep cuts and the finer tracery. Stone wheels next smoothed the roughly cut surfaces.

"Wooden wheels with pumice and water gave an approach to a polish, and finally rapidly revolving brushes with putty powder (tin oxide) gave a high finish. The men who operated these four types of apparatus were all highly skilled and highly paid. About 1895 attempts were made to utilize the action of hydrofluoric acid on glass in order to eliminate the two final processes almost entirely. Many difficulties were encountered by the chemists who attempted to control this reaction.

"Finally, however, they were overcome, and one or two men can now polish the output of a large factory, permitting the laying off of perhaps forty highly paid workers, and the selling to the public of fine cut-glass ware at much less than it could otherwise be marketed."

During the last fifty years the two most important influences in the manufacture of glass were, first, the substitution of gas for coal, and second, the invention

Fig. 1.  GREEK BOTTLE
5th Century B.C.

Fig. 2.  GREEK BOTTLE

*(See page 5)*

[ 15 ]

Fig. 3.  SARACENIC VASE

(*See page* 6)

Fig. 4.  PERSIAN GLASS
18th Century.

(*See page 6*)

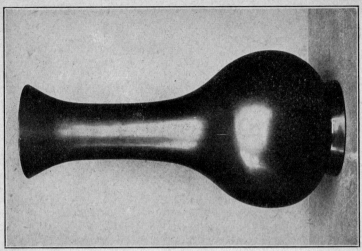

Fig. 6. CHINESE VASE

Fig. 5. CHINESE VASE

(*See page 7*)

Fig. 7. VENETIAN COVERED CUP

(See page 30)

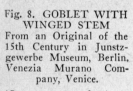

Fig. 8. GOBLET WITH
WINGED STEM
From an Original of the
15th Century in Junstz-
gewerbe Museum, Berlin.
Venezia Murano Com-
pany, Venice.

(*See pages* 32 *and* 33)

Fig. 9. VENETIAN TAZZA
From 15th Century Original in the Morosini Gallery, Venice.

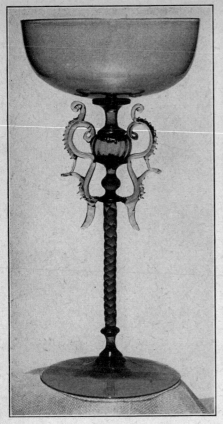

Fig. 10.   GOBLET WITH WINGED
STEM
From an Original of the 15th Century in
the British Museum.

(*See pages* 34 *and* 36)

Fig. 11.   VITRO DI
TRINA WINE GLASS
Vitro di Trina Glass
from Original of the 15th
Century in the Murano
Museum.

Fig. 12. BASIN AND EWER
Italian, 16th Century.

(*See page* 37)

of the glass-blowing machine.*　This machine was invented by M. J. Owens, of Toledo, Ohio, and of course, revolutionised the making of glass.　Modern glass moulds are of three kinds, iron, press and paste moulds, all of them made of iron.　These moulds are made in two or more segments fastened together, and no matter how well they are made, wear and tear and abuse in using them makes the joint of the mould apparent.

The Germans used moulds of maple or apple wood soaked in water.　After use the moulds grew charred on the inside, and the blower found that the object within could be easily revolved, giving it a lustre and smoothing off the seams.　Iron moulds in use at the time if covered on the inside with some of the charred mixture from the wooden moulds, allowed the object to be revolved as in the wooden moulds.　This gradually led to a carbon mixture being known as "paste."

The writer of "Fifty Years of Glass Making" goes on to say that this paste mixture is applied on the inside of a mould, and often sprayed with water so it will not burn.　A paste mould of this description will not allow an object with a raised design upon it to be treated in this way.　A "press" mould is made of two parts, the mould and the plunger, the mould being the outer part and the plunger working within it.　The press operator gathers a bit of molten glass on the punty, drops it in the mould, shears it away from the punty, and presses

* "Fifty Years of Glass Making."

in the plunger. The press operator must have an accurate eye to judge of the right amount of metal so it will not be too much to fill the mould, and so be wasted, or too little which will cause under pressing.

The styles of decoration are many:

*Cutting.* This was among the earliest methods used, and is one of the most beautiful. It was accomplished by the use of wheels from two to sixteen inches in diameter, sand, water, powdered pumice, and "putty powder," consisting of whitening and other ingredients, for polishing. The wheels were of blue stone, mild steel or hard wood, boxwood generally for polishing. The cutter revolved the wheels by foot power, pressed the glass against the wheel on which sand and water dripped. The design was rudely scratched on the glass and then the cutter followed the details from a sketch on paper which lay beside him.

*Diamond-point engraving.* This style of decorating was employed long before the use of the wheel. Every country where glass was made used it, and as late as the middle of the nineteenth century it was still employed in England.

*Engraving by wheel.* This method followed the diamond-point style. The effect if done by an artist was often extremely rich. One cannot study or handle glass without noting the frequent use of the grapevine as an ornament. With or without the bunch of grapes which so often accompany it, its use was not confined by any means to drinking vessels. The grace of the stem, the curling tendrils, the pleasing shape of the leaf, made it adaptable to objects of any form. I have found it on glass vessels of every description except perhaps salt-cellars.

A very agreeable variation of engraved glass is found when a portion of the pattern is left clear and polished. Besides the vine and the hop and barley sprays found on ale glasses, flowers were favorite designs. Tulip, rose and lily, honeysuckle and leaf vine, all had their place; the tulip in particular, beloved of the Dutch, often figured on glass from the Low Countries.

*Fluoric Acid Etching.* This art, which originated in Germany, had in the eighteenth century many followers in England. Their productions were among the most exquisite which it is possible to produce upon glass, seeming hardly more than a shadow of a design blown upon the glass.

*Flashing.* This is superimposing upon clear glass a thin layer of coloured glass. This layer of coloured glass can be used either upon the inside or outside of the clear glass. When cut through for purposes of decoration the result of flashing on the inside shows clear figures on a coloured background, while coloured figures on a clear ground are the result of applying the coloured glass on the outside.

*Trailing.* Canes or rods of glass laid on in a pattern while the metal was still hot, makes a somewhat clumsy but effective decoration. It was commonly combined with etching or engraving.

In Rosenhain's "Glass Making in All Ages," he says: "The blowing of a tumbler is typical of the process of blowing any hollow article, and the higher grade the object the more depends on the skill of the worker. The old way of forming a tumbler was to take the gathering of glass on the blowpipe, blowing it into the proper size, then elongating by gently swinging the pipe. Then the bottom was flattened by pressing it gently on the marver, which gave the tumbler the proper shape. The pontil was affixed to the bottom by a small bit of glass, the neck and blowpipe were separated from the bulb, leaving the tumbler the proper size. The edge of the tumbler was thrust into the furnace to heat the broken edge, which was now smoothed and rounded off. If the worker so desired the edge could be widened out or fluted, or otherwise treated by rotating it, and pressing the edge with pieces of wood."

When you come to consider the collecting of old glass, one of the most discouraging things to be faced is the number of frauds and fakes. Not only is old Irish and English glass being forged, but early American as well. Often the highest precautions will not defend the purchaser. In the presence of the pontil mark collectors once used to place their trust, but this is no longer an infallible test. Old cut-glass of high quality generally did have the pontil mark smoothed off, and so did many pieces which were not cut.

The form of the foot in drinking glasses is a means of identifying old pieces. It is generally large, the diameter being equal to that of the bowl, and it is conical or domed. The bottom of old pieces is frequently like ground glass, and always has at least a rim of wear around its edge.

There are collectors who claim that they can never be deceived in the "ring" of old glass. That is, if the rim of the object is struck smartly with a pencil or the fingernail it gives out a clear, musical note. I have before me a large, dark-blue beaker which rings clear and true when struck. Yet it is an unmistakable fake. It is thick and heavy, it is a bad shade of blue, and the bottom has been industriously scratched with sandpaper. Not content with this, there are some extra-large scratches made no doubt with a file. On a genuine piece the wear shows evenly, coming from use and moving about. Most of the old glass was less clear and brilliant than the modern. It had many imperfections in it, tiny bubbles, sometimes little grains of sand, which Mrs. Stannus in "Old Irish Glass" says is one of the peculiarities of old Irish glass.

Constant handling of old glass is a most necessary part of the training of every would-be collector. Old glass lacks the sharpness of new, there is a feeling of softness almost as noticeable as in soft paste porcelain, and sometimes the fingers will be more of an aid to you in detecting the fraud, than the eyes.

THE making of glass before it became so mechanical a process as it is now, was one of the most beautiful arts in the world. The glass-worker could please his fancy in the shape and decoration of the objects he fashioned, and the greater variety of form he introduced, the better it was.

The story of Venice, the history of her proud nobles with their wealth of ducats and their ropes of pearls, is like a fairy tale. For centuries those oozy quicksands were the nesting-grounds of wild birds, and the sea was choked with fishes. Then by and by came men and women, driven to such fastnesses as the lagunes provided by the raids of the Goths. They fought the sea, building up with wooden piles driven deep into the shifting sand, and men, women and children toiled to give stability to the ooze and silt.

By degrees the rude mud huts gave way to cottages, and these in turn to more substantial dwellings, though the fierce daily battle went on to keep the water out and retain the shallow strips of soil. The best men in each little knot of dwellings were chosen as leaders, and little by little the process of selection showed its advantages. Invention and the creative faculty seems to have been inborn in them, they were Christians too, and in 421 A.D., Rivo-Alto (the Rialto), or Port of Padua as it was called, sent consuls to regulate the lives and property of the water settlers, and to safeguard them from the inroads of barbarians.*

The first "Grand" Doge of Venice was Agnello Badoero, a Greek by descent, who was called to the supreme office in 810, and he chose Rivo-Alto as the seat of government, and set about developing and improving the islands of the lagunes.†

It would seem but natural that a race sprung from fisherfolk and toilers should lack, not excel, in all lines of art. But touch them where you will, even the simplest things were wrought on lines of beauty, and their artists, printers, goldsmiths, weavers of rich lace and splendid textiles, makers of glass and mosaics, seemed to draw inspiration from the colours and forms they found in their wonderful gardens or shimmering on the surrounding waters.

Glass-making was early an important Italian industry. From the fifth century there are records of it, the artisans working in a small way at little individual furnaces, instead of in the immense establishments of more modern times. The earliest recorded individual worker was Petrus Flavianus, in the year 1090, as a phial maker.‡

In 1268 the glass-workers became an incorporated

* Staley: "Dogaressas of Venice."
† Charles Yriate: "Venice."
‡ Monograph on Venice and the Island of Murano.

body, and took part in processions and pageants. Glass for windows and mirrors and vessels of glass for household use were all made as early as the fourteenth century, and during the sixteenth and seventeenth centuries immense quantities were exported. Figure 7 shows one of the splendid covered cups of the fifteenth century. It is of plain glass, the bowl, the cover and the foot ornamented with raised gadroons and ribs. Around the mouth is a band of enamelled dots on a gold ground, and beneath that a raised rib, coloured spirally blue and white. Around the bottom of the cup is a raised moulded band. It belongs to the end of the fifteenth century, and is in the Victoria and Albert Museum, London.

The seat of this prosperous industry was the Island of Murano, whither the workers had been transferred late in the twelfth century. It is a fact that glass-works had been established at Treviso, Ravenna, Vicenza, Padua, Mantua, and Bologna by the end of the thirteenth century, but they were so overshadowed by Venice that little is known of them, or what they made.

The Island of Murano, separated from Venice by an arm of the sea, was not only celebrated on account of the glass-works which were gathered together there. For years it was the abode of the aristocrats of Venice, and here they built their gardens, and many villas sprang up on the sandy seashore, whose hanging gar-

*Figure 7, page 19.*

dens and orchard terraces were claimed to be the most beautiful in the world.

During the fifteenth and sixteenth centuries when these villas were at their proudest, every visitor extolled the beauty of the gardens snatched from the sea. Every afternoon and evening fleets of gondolas stole through the murky waters, filled with merry people who went to Murano to enjoy the cool breezes filled with the scent of flowers, or to view the splendid frescoes and wonderful statuary at Villa Mocenigo and Villa Trevison.*

But while the nobles had complete liberty to go and come as they pleased, the glass-workers were virtually imprisoned there so that the secrets of the manufacture should not become known. But to reward them for this curtailment of liberty they had astonishing privileges. They were under the immediate jurisdiction of the Council of Ten, and they had the right of coining a certain number of medals on the day of the blessing of the waters by the Doge. If one of their daughters married a noble the latter did not forfeit his nobility, and the children were noble. A very great concession in those days.† If, however, one of the workers attempted to leave the island, he was punished with death.

The number and variety of guilds at Venice seems

* Staley: "Dogaressas of Venice."
† Yriate: "Venice."

to have embraced every known occupation. In the splendid pageants which were such a feature of Venetian life for centuries, it was customary for the different guilds to appear, generally in rich uniforms and bearing show-pieces illustrative of their trade. Each branch of the glass-makers' trade had its own guild, and they were divided into mirror makers, crystal glass workers, mosaic glass workers, and bead makers. These latter were divided into ordinary bead makers and bead makers of finer quality.*

During the reign of Doge Giovanni Soranzo (1312-29), and Dogaressa Franchesina his wife, importations of mirrors from Germany and hanging lamps from Greece were prohibited. Their palace was one of the grandest in Venice, filled with costly treasures, with table service of gold and silver-gilt and the most beautiful glass Murano could produce. No doubt tall goblets similar to the one shown in Figure 8 stood on their table, for this one is a copy of one in the Berlin Museum, and is in the Pennsylvania Museum, Philadelphia. The original is of the fifteenth century. The exquisite lines of these tall goblets, the admirable proportion, the delicacy of the winged ornament, belonged more to the fifteenth and sixteenth centuries than later when the ornament became too heavy, and in some cases almost grotesque.

During the years 1547-49, discontent raged among

* Dillon: "Glass."
*Figure 8, page 20.*

the glass workers of Murano. Instead of asking for less time to work—the modern method—they complained that so much time was taken by observances of church and state, and the restrictions of labour under legal enactments, that the working year was reduced to thirty-five weeks. Luigi Conaro in his "Discorso Intorno Alla Vita Sobria," has recorded: "Cloth of gold from India, porcelain and glass from Sèvres, earthenware from Birmingham, and other manufactures entered Venice freely to the disadvantage of Venetian workmen." The Gastaldi or Masters of the Guild laid their complaints before the Dogaressa Alicia, and she was able to obtain permission in 1550 for a party of Murano glass-workers to travel through England, Flanders, Spain and France. King Henry VIII of England welcomed them and made a great collection of Venetian glass.

Among the exquisite objects made were tazze—one is shown in Figure 9. They are flat, shallow bowls mounted on stems and very often flecked or powdered with gold. The one shown is at the Pennsylvania Museum, and is a copy of one in the Morosini Gallery at Venice. It belongs to the fifteenth century.

Slender, long-necked bottles for water were made in quantities at the furnaces of the Miotti and Luna families. Their glass was colourless, not very brilliant, but ornamented with ribs and rings of white enamel.*

*Ryley: "Old Venetian Glass."
*Figure 9, page 20.*

The glasses of the sixteenth and seventeenth centuries are very beautiful, and may have funnel-shaped bowls, fluted, four-leaved, scalloped, or tulip-shaped. The latter is very pleasing, particularly when decorated with ribs and threads of glass. Many of these early glasses were colourless, but there are some of a royal purple that are exceptionally fine. The Venetians had a fancy for lavishing decoration on the stems, which were often fourteen inches high. They are balustered, winged, crested with glass of another colour, twisted and ringed in endless variety. Figure 10 is from an original glass of the fifteenth century which is in the British Museum, London. This replica is at the Pennsylvania Museum, Philadelphia. Everything about this glass is interesting. The tall braided stem, the winged decoration which is so suggestive of the sea-horse, a design which has always seemed to appeal to glass-makers, American as well as European.

The importance of Altare, a small Ligurian town north of Savona, has only recently been recognised as having an important part in the development of the glass industry of the sixteenth century. As far back as the eleventh century a glass industry had been established there, and there was a constant influx of skilled workmen from Normandy and later from Murano, so that by the fifteenth century there were so many trained workers that they were ready to go to other countries to seek employment. Constantly from this

*Figure 10, page 21.*

time Altare has played an important part in this art, does so to-day, for there are descendants of the old families—Mr. Dillon in his book, "Glass," says thirteen—who still carry on the craft.

The term "Venetian Glass" always conjures up in the mind those lovely and fragile objects with which we are familiar. But the earliest glass was made for the mosaic makers to use. Then about the beginning of the fourteenth century they made lanterns for galleys and lighthouses. They made glass in blocks for spectacle makers, mosaic glass, window glass, glass for mirrors, each branch of the work being under its own code of laws which bound both master and workmen.*

Salvino d'Amato invented eye-glasses towards the end of the thirteenth century, and they were subsequently improved by Allessandro Spina.†

About 1436 the coloured glass of Venice began to be celebrated, and continued so for centuries. By the fifteenth and continuing to the sixteenth centuries plain glass decorated with gilt and enamel was much esteemed; while in the seventeenth century the celebrated vitro di trina, marbled and variegated glass were all being made. Millefiori extends through all periods.‡

The enamelled glass of the sixteenth century was very beautiful, and the imitations of jasper, agate and chalcedony very successful. The vitro di trina or lace-

* "The Americana."
† Wallace-Dunlop: "Glass in the Old World."
‡ Apsley Pellatt: "Curiosities of Glass Making."

glass consists of fine threads of white or opaque glass contained in the body glass. They might be vertical or horizontal, and might appear in the form of ribs or bands. Figure 11 shows a vase, vitro di trina of the fifteenth century, a copy of one in the Murano Museum. This one is at the Pennsylvania Museum, and is exceedingly beautiful and graceful.

As the seventeenth century advanced, the style became florid and gaudy, particularly in such objects as chandeliers and wall lights. Many formulas were used for the composition and colouring of the old glass, the colouring particularly being a very delicate matter, since it depended not only upon the just proportion of the ingredients, but upon the greatest care in the application of heat. The choicest specimens were sometimes submitted to the heat fifty or sixty times.*

There are a few great names connected with the making of glass in Venice: Ballarin; the leaders of the schools of Brussa and Briati, particularly Guiseppe Briati himself, who in 1736 obtained a patent to make glass in Venice in the Bohemian style. He had learned the secret of its manufacture at Prague. He also was allowed to set up his furnace in Venice itself, in the Via del Angelo Raffaello, in 1739, and destroyed those he had at Murano. He died in 1772.†

Another of the illustrious of Venetian glass-makers

*Yriate: "Venice."
† Ibid.
Figure 11, page 21.

was Angelo Beroviero, who, with members of his family, made many improvements in glass-making. In 1463 they invented what they called "crystal glass," and from it they made those wonderful cups and goblets which were used as marriage or betrothal gifts; they also made memorial vases and show-pieces for the guild. These latter were sumptuous objects, rich with gold and enamel decoration, and in some cases showed historical portraits. The ewer and basin in Figure 12 show the grace which such masters of their craft bestowed upon everything they touched. These pieces are in the Victoria and Albert Museum, London, and are of clear glass banded with blue.

Angelo Beroviero, aided by his friend Paolo Godi da Pergola, a chemist, was able to manufacture artificial gems as well as artificial pearls.*

Anyone who has read much of the ancient history of Venice as well as other parts of Italy, is staggered at the amount of jewels mentioned. "Pounds of Great Pearls" figure in inventories of estates and in accounts of the wealth and marriage portions of great ladies of noble rank. A. Sauzay in his "Wonders of Glass Making," says: "On his return to Venice (1295) Marco Polo hastened to inform his fellow citizens who were dauntless mariners as well as enterprising merchants, not only of the manners, but also of the taste of the people of Tartary, India, and China for false pearls

* Sauzay: "Wonders of Glass Making."
*Figure 12, page 22.*

and imitation gems. Nothing more was required to exercise the inventive mind of the Venetians. Thus while Dominico Miotti endowed Venice with the invention of blowing false pearls which had been lost for centuries, Christopher Briati, on his side, revived an art once carried to great perfection, the production of coloured glass and aventurine. Such efforts necessarily brought their rewards, and it is to the pearls and coloured glass in the imitation of precious stones, that Venice owed in great part the wealth she gained from both hemispheres."

The pearls are made from tubes of glass, the thickness of the tube being in proportion to its size. After the end of the tube is blown into a ball-shape, it has to be twice pierced, if for stringing; is further modelled into shape, round or pear shape; and then coloured. This colouring is introduced into the interior of the glass globe after a slight coating of glue has been sprayed over the inside, and is a powder made of fish-scales. Previous to 1686 the colouring matter was made of quicksilver. The work of colouring these pearls was done by women, a skillful worker finishing about forty thousand a day.

Although those past-masters of the arts, the Egyptians, made false pearls fifteen centuries before our era, Pliny says that the taste for fine pearls was introduced into Rome by Pompeius Magnus about 693 A.D. He did not stint himself in the use of these gems, for even

Fig. 13.  DRINKING VESSELS AND EWER
Venetian.
Fig. 15.  BOHEMIAN GLASS, DIAMOND ENGRAVED
(See pages 50 and 52)

[ 39 ]

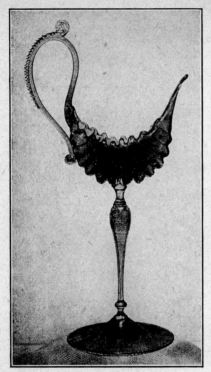

Fig. 14. VENETIAN VASE
Venice, 19th Century.

Fig. 16. BOHEMIAN
GLASS, PAINTED
Clear Glass, Cylindrical,
Painted with Two Coats of
Arms, an Inscription in Gilt
and the Date 1868.

(*See pages* 50 *and* 53)

Fig. 17.  COVERED GOBLET

Goblet with Cover, Green Glass, Engraved, and with an Inscription.
A Silver-gilt Openwork Foot, and on the Cover Silver-gilt Figure of a
Dog Standing, with the Initials I. A. V. and the Date 1656.

(*See page* 54)

Fig. 18. DEEP-CUT      Fig. 19. KALLIGRAPHEN
TUMBLER          ORNAMENTE

Fig. 20. DOPPELWANDGLAS

(*See pages* 55 *and* 57)

Fig. 21.  MILCH GLASS, PAINTED
Fig. 23.  BOHEMIAN DECANTERS
(*See pages 57 and 58*)

**Fig 22. COVERED CUPS**
Bohemian Glass Covered Cups. Metropolitan Museum of Art.
(*See page* 58)

Fig. 24. BEHERSCREW,
SILVER-GILT
Dutch Beherscrew, Silver-gilt. 17th
Century. Property of the City of
Amsterdam.

(*See pages* 71 *and* 72)

Fig. 25. DUTCH WINDMILL
GLASS
Dutch Mill Beher. Latticinio **and**
Silver. 17th Century.

Fig. 26.  DUTCH GLASS, VENETIAN STYLE
With Diamond Engraving, 17th Century.

Fig. 27.  DIAMOND-ENGRAVED GLASS
Green Glass, Dutch Diamond Engraving, 1646.

(*See page* 73)

his furniture was studded with them. There was a likeness of himself wrought entirely in pearls, and he had besides chaplets and ornaments.

Of course such a spendthrift and dandy as Caligula could not be outdone in magnificence, so he had his shoes decorated with pearls. His horse, Incitatus, had his collar studded with them, and they were used in countless other ways. These were Oriental pearls, and of course only obtainable by the wealthy. Twenty years after Marco Polo brought news that false pearls were desired in India and China, there were so many makers of these gewgaws that they were regulated by special statute.

The mirrors of Venice were for long years objects of envy by the rest of the world, and on these and the making of beads they had a monopoly. The making of mirrors requires not only a good plate of glass free from all imperfections, but the applying of a film of bright metal, which shall be free from all defects. The mirrors of the fifteenth and sixteenth centuries were always small, not alone from the fact that it was not then possible to make large sheets of glass, but also because in the hands of a Renaissance artist, the frame was the important thing. Whether of gold, jewelled, or of carved wood, or tortoise-shell inlaid or rich with lapis, it was a masterpiece, and the mirror was only an excuse for all this enrichment. The little mirrors which women wore were small things indeed, worn generally at the girdle. They were often about four inches high by two wide in an embossed frame, or if round, were commonly enclosed in a small ivory box richly carved.

When England began to make mirrors the business in them was dropped in Venice, so that by 1772 only one glass house at Murano made them.*

In addition to the desire for false pearls and imitation gems, the feminine rage for beads does not seem to have lessened with years. If there were documents concerning the manners and customs of Adam and Eve, how they kept house and what they wore when they walked out of an afternoon, there is no doubt in my mind but that reference would be found to chains of rowan beads and hips and haws, with which they decked themselves.

Nobody knows how far back the making of beads began in Egypt, for beads of colour—sapphire, emerald and brown—were well known by the time of the XVIIIth Dynasty, that is from 1500-1350 B.C. The skill of the Egyptian women in making exquisite adornments out of beads can be seen in the Egyptian room of any great museum. The small thin chains which satisfy us to-day are meagre compared to the splendid and artistic breastplates and collars of Egyptian make. Even the melancholy bugle bead, so well known as the jangling accompaniment to modified mourning, has

* Yriate: "Venice."

been used for centuries and centuries for the same purpose.

Gabrielle d'Estrees, Marquise de Monceaux, mistress of Henry IV of France, died in 1599. In her inventory are noted "Five small caps of black satin of which two are embroidered in jet, one quite full, a robe of black satin with a border of jet over the body and the sleeves open, valued at forty crowns." *

In 1723 Savary wrote in his "Dictionnaire Universel du Commerce": "It is with artificial jet, cut and pierced and threaded with silk or thread, that embroideries are made in sufficiently good taste, but very dear, which are used particularly in churches. Trimmings are also made of it in half mourning for men and women, and sometimes muffs and tippets, and trimmings for robes."

The tons of glass beads which are worn by women in every part of the world to-day, be the women black, white, yellow or red, seems only the outcropping of a desire for flashy adornment, which is ingrained in the feminine nature. The modern bead may be more regular, but often it is far less beautiful than its predecessor of centuries ago.

The Chevron bead is perhaps the most important of all Venetian beads, not alone on account of its size, but because of its wide distribution. These beads are made from canes built up from layers of colored glass, gen-

* Sauzay.

erally, blue, red, and green, divided by thin layers of opaque white glass which are so placed that the opaque glass forms a star-like pattern on a cross-section. They vary in size from one-third of an inch to two and a half inches, and the usual type is cylindrical with rounded ends. These beads are very beautiful, and have been made at Murano so long that the time of their introduction is unknown. They are made at the present time in large quantities for use in the Congo, where they are in great demand.

They have been found in the remotest spots of the earth, Upper Egypt and Nubia, Zanzibar and India, Central Africa, South Sea Islands, Peru, Canada, and even in the graves of the American Indians.*

Thinking of Murano as one of the greatest artistic colonies in the world, it seems unbelievable to know that they had to have recourse to making ugly and common things. Yet in 1790 Giorgio Barbaria asks for a patent for making black bottles for export to England, and also enamels and jet. His is the last great name in the industry of glass-making at Murano. He was deputy of the Island for 1794-96, and this was just before the republic fell. Murano once so proud and prosperous came on evil days, and though the art is still carried on, it is done so by foreigners, or at least on foreign capital.† See figures 13 and 14.

* Dillon: "Glass."
† Yriate: "Venice."
*Figures 13 and 14, pages 39-40.*

THE glass industry was introduced into Bohemia from Venice, in the thirteenth century, and soon attained a vast importance. The glass factories were in the neighbourhood of the mountains, where minerals, especially silica, abounded, and where fuel was plentiful.

The finest product, the crystal glass, is to-day made around Haida and Steinschonau, the same places where the art originally flourished. When one nowadays speaks of Bohemian glass, there flashes instantly into the mind a not too agreeable shade of red, with a decoration of vine leaves and grapes in white.

But this glass is not the one for which the works in Bohemia became famous. That was a glass crystal clear, artistic in its shape and very similar to the Venetian glass from which it was copied. The heyday of this beautiful product was the seventeenth century, when, under the fostering care of the Emperor Ferdinand III, the elder and younger Schwanhardt of Nuremberg turned out their masterpieces.*

The art of cutting was really derived from the art of rock-crystal cutting, imported into Italy after the conquest of Constantinople, in 1453. From Italy it

* Ryley: "Old Bohemian Glass."

passed into Nuremberg about 1550, and then into Prague. The recluse Rudolph II was a great patron of the arts, and encouraged the glass industry by inviting to come to his castle at Prague such celebrated lapidaries as he could hear of. Chief among these were Girlamo and Gaspardo Miseroni, who came from Milan and were placed in charge of a glass-works, which had been founded by Rudolph himself.*

The decoration of Venetian glass of this period was far from artistic. It was either scratched with a diamond or painted in enamels. The beautiful glass made at Prague and Nuremberg still showed the influence of Albrecht Dürer (he died 1528), for at this time and for many years after, these two cities were the headquarters of science and art. The glass itself, much improved in quality and clearness by the use of potassium carbonate instead of sodium carbonate, was cut with the same care as rock-crystal. The deep cutting was done with the apex of the natural crystal, while the lighter etching was made with a splinter or fragment of a diamond.

Figure 15 shows a group of this diamond-etched glass, of the sixteenth century. The elegant shapes of the vessels themselves and the grace of the decorations are far more Italian in character than many other pieces of about the same period. In fact the demand of the customers was responsible for the character of

* Ryley: "Old Bohemian Glass."
Figure 15, page 39.

the glass. A great contrast to these pieces is shown in Figure 16. This is a tall drinking glass very German in shape, size and enamelled decoration. There are two coats of arms on it in colour, and an inscription with the date 1568. This glass is owned by the Victoria and Albert Museum, London.

Bohemian glass, even of the choicer qualities, was not always blown. The heavier pieces which were to be subjected to the deep cutting were cast in wooden moulds. The wheels dressed with emery and diamond dust which are used by lapidaries at the present day were used by the early cutters in Bohemia, who soon abandoned, except for polishing, the primitive sandstone or wood and metal wheels. A. Beresford Ryley in his paper on "Old Bohemian Glass," in the *Connoisseur,* says that George Schwanhardt and his son Henry, both of Nuremberg, were never excelled or even equalled in the beauty and delicacy of their work. The elder Schwanhardt was a pupil and assistant of Caspar Lehmann, who had learned his art at Prague under the two Miseroni. The Thirty Years' War desolated Bohemia and Schwanhardt returned to Nuremberg, from which city he had gone to Prague to be director of the Imperial furnaces.

From Nuremberg came many of his marvellous masterpieces. Princes of the church quarrelled with Royalty for possession of his glasses, and finally, owing to the entreaties of the Emperor Ferdinand III, he re-

*Figure 16, page 40.*

turned to Prague. Under his direction his models were copied in the various glass-works. His return to Prague was in the year 1652, and he and his son Henry continued to do their marvellous work on goblets, tankards, tumblers and beakers. The "pokale," or goblets, often with tall graceful covers, were especially elegant. Sometimes these goblets in addition to being facetted and cut were practically covered with engraving, and even then might be further embellished with gold rims and stands. Figure 17 shows a splendid example of such a covered cup. It is of clear green glass, engraved and with an inscription. A silver-gilt openwork foot and on the cover a silver-gilt dog, standing, further enrich it. It also bears the initials I. A.V. and the date 1656. This cup is at the Victoria and Albert Museum, London.

During the last half of the seventeenth century the celebrated ruby glass began to make its appearance. It was brought to perfection about 1679 by Johann Kunckel, a Silesian, at his glass-works on the Isle of Peacocks, at Pottsdam. Kunckel, born 1638, was at first a chemist, and his researches led him to investigate the colouring of glass. He detected the fact that to get this wonderful shade of ruby the glass had to be twice heated, and that the gold, used as colouring, must be present only in minute quantities.*

A little book called "L'Arte Vetraria," published by

* Dillon: "Glass."
*Figure 17, page 41.*

Antonio Neri in 1612, has had an important influence
on both makers of glass and on writers on that subject. This book passed through four translations, re-
ceiving valuable additions each time. It was translated
first from Italian to English, then to Latin, to German
and finally to French, which latter translation, by
Baron d'Hollack in Paris, 1752, is the best.

Much of this deeply cut Bohemian glass, modern as
well as antique, is very heavy. This is necessary on
account of the style of decoration, deep-cutting, "tief-
geschnitten," and an example of this glass is shown in
Figure 18. Fruit and figures, horns of plenty, with
inscriptions and quite a medley of objects crowded
together, gives a showy but less artistic decoration than
some of the simpler pieces. Usually, the main object, a
portrait, a picture of a town, which was a favourite subject, a bunch of flowers or fruit, or even an elaborate
geometric design was deeply cut while the lesser parts,
scrolls, curlicues, swags and tendrils were done in much
lower relief, often etched.

During the first half of the eighteenth century, a
mode of decoration called "kalligraphen ornamente"
was much admired. It was extremely beautiful, light
and elegant scroll-work and conventional decoration
which practically covered the whole object. Figure
19 shows it. It is no wonder that the demand for this
exquisite product increased and spread all over Europe,

*Figures 18 and 19, page 42.*

particularly in those centres where the elegancies of life were in demand.

Maria Theresa, Countess of Flanders, visited Ghent in 1744, which city had been hitherto a market for Venetian glass. In fact much glass made in Ghent had been directly copied from Venetian models. But the glasses made to celebrate Maria Theresa's visit were in Bohemian style, rich with engraved armorial bearings.*

Indeed, about the middle of the eighteenth century, the demand for this glass in Bohemian style had a disastrous effect on Venetian manufactures. Though the glass-works at Murano were nearly ruined, the Senate forbade them to make any goods in Bohemian style. Things grew so bad at last that in 1736 the Senate granted permission to Guiseppe Briati to establish in Venice a furnace to make glass in Bohemian style. Briati himself was a Muranese glass-maker who had studied the art of Bohemian glass-making secretly at Prague. Some of his models are still to be seen at the Murano Museum. These pieces of Briati are most interesting. Into the shapes he succeeded in imparting a lightness not to be found in the solid and imposing pieces of Bohemian design. The quality of the glass was more brilliant and clearer than that previously made at Murano. His cups and beakers were of an elegance and beauty that made them treasured by all who gained possession of them. At the Doge's palace

* Sauzay: "Wonders of Glass Making."

they were displayed on the cupboards among the gold and silver plate.*

Later in the eighteenth century, a new style of work called "Doppelwandglas" was produced in Bohemia. Specimens are shown in Figure 20. This Doppelwandglas was a revival of an ancient art practised long before. The objects made in it were commonly goblets or bowls, very heavy, with round or square bases. They were made of two layers of glass, holding between them the decoration etched in gold or silver leaf. Sometimes the inner layer was of ruby glass, but oftener of clear, the two layers fastened together by a colorless cement, or by fusion, the inner layer of glass being very fusible, so that a low degree of heat would attach it hermetically to the outer layer.

The effect was often very brilliant and beautiful, particularly if the design was kept simple. But as the Bohemian glass ousted the Venetian, so English flint glass with its marvellous power of decomposing light owing to the presence of lead, ousted Bohemian.

Searching for novelties the Bohemian workers not only imposed black silhouettes on backgrounds of gold or silver, but they also returned to painted glass, the background of which was whitish glass. This they called "Milchglas," and some of it is shown in Figure 21. Some of these painted designs are most attractive, par-

* Yriate: "Venice."
*Figures 20 and 21, pages 42 and 43.*

ticularly on the early pieces, but late in the century the taste became rococo, and nothing was too gaudy.

Early in 1800 in an effort to revive the industry quantities of ruby glass were made. Some is shown in Figure 22. There were smaller lots made of blue, amber, and very rarely green. These were often in two layers, milk-white over a colour, in which the opaque glass was cut through to show the colour beneath. Sometimes thumb-spots was the pattern chosen, sometimes the colour layer was cut through to show clear glass. Such pieces are by no means rare in this country, particularly in the coarser qualities. Some are shown in Figure 23.

The map of Europe has been so juggled with that one hardly dares to state the domain of Bohemia. There are, however, six principal glass-making centres in Bohemia or adjacent to it. Of these Haida ranks first, and was in the business as early as the thirteenth century.

The method of glass-making in Bohemia up to 1870 and indeed for ten years later (see 10th Census of the United States) was most primitive. All the furnaces throughout Austria-Hungary were small affairs placed in the midst of forests, and when the wood near at hand was exhausted it was found cheaper to move the furnaces than to bring wood. The way the manufacture was conducted was almost as primitive as the works. The work was divided into two distinct branches, one

*Figures 22 and 23, pages 43 and 44.*

where the rough unfinished glass was made, and the other the refining or finishing, which included engraving or decorating of the crude article.

This method caused the training of a band of skilled workmen, excellent engravers and decorators. They were further encouraged by a government museum, and schools were maintained in connection with the glass industry where art training could be obtained. In 1880 there were in Bohemia alone 169 furnaces making glass, most of them making crystal, table, hollow ware, coloured glasses, bottles and other fine ware. They also made glass pipes for beads, glass sticks, cut glass and coloured raw glass. Only twelve of these furnaces used coal. The quantity of Bohemian glass sent to this country was perfectly immense. The tables showing the imports of glass into the United States between the years 1876-80, under the head of "Bohemian, cut, engraved, painted, coloured, printed, stained, silvered or gilded, plain, mold and pressed," was valued at $2,972,089.76. No wonder there is plenty of it to be found, and that it makes its frequent appearance at auctions.

Glatz has a great reputation at the present time as a glass-making centre and these Bohemian glass-works send their products all over the world, Africa as well as America demanding them. They are making now some exceptionally beautiful coloured glass of the highest quality, in the old shapes, "tief-geschnitten," and consequently very expensive. Pieces in a gorgeous amber or in the fine clear red, tall covered cups and vases also with covers can be found and are most decorative. Many of them bear a label which reads, "Made in Czecho-Slovakia."

In studying up the early history of Bohemian glass, it was soon apparent that like so many other industries and arts, its beginnings were very foggy. But in the Congressional Library in Washington, that Mecca of all students who try to delve into antique history, I found in one of the card catalogues a book entitled "Bohemian Glass." It seemed as if my almost hopeless searches were about to be rewarded. So vast is the library and so distant some of the stack-rooms, that you are requested by frequent signs not to ask, under half an hour, if your book has come. Just sit down and wait patiently, and if your book is in an attendant will bring it to you. I waited the half-hour and some over, though to me patience has always seemed a poor kind of virtue. The librarian who finally answered, said "Bohemian Glass" was an "art book," and was to be found on the third floor at the end of the print room. An art book, how promising that sounded! To get to the print room was a walk equivalent to several city blocks in length and on arrival at the desk one of the very polite and helpful women who attend to the wants of readers, said she did not know the book but would have it looked for. So there was more waiting, quite watchful waiting this time, and she presently arrived at my side with a very doubtful look and a very small book. She remarked that she feared the book would hardly serve my purpose, and put it in my hand.

"Bohemian Glass" was a book of poems published in Oxford, England. It was declared to be one of "Works of Authors Unknown to Fame," which on looking through the volume was quite understandable. However, I copied the following lines, as forming one of the shortest and most lucid gems!

*"Of a Certain Green-eyed Monster."*

"Charles gave Elizabeth a Dodo,
Charles never offered one to me—
The loveliest lemon-coloured Dodo
With the greenest eyes that you could wish to see.

Now it isn't that I'm doubting if Charles loves me,
And I know he would ask me out to tea,
But he did give Elizabeth a Dodo,
And he never even offered one to me."

THE political history of what is now known as The Netherlands, and Belgium, seems to have been linked with nearly every country in Europe. They have been included in the Holy Roman Empire, they have been ruled by French kings. The Dukes of Burgundy fostered their arts and the country prospered, but when The Netherlands passed with King Philip II to the Spanish line of the House of Hapsburg, its domain was considerably reduced.

In 1795 Flanders, like other provinces of Belgium, was incorporated with the French Republic, but the Congress of Vienna united Belgium and Holland to form the Kingdom of The Netherlands. Not till 1830-32 did Belgium liberate itself from Holland. The glass-workers travelled from one city and country to another, and it is difficult to classify glass which has so strong a family resemblance, as being distinctively Flemish or Dutch, particularly when both Venice and Germany exerted so strong an influence on this art in both Belgium and Holland. It was but natural that the workmen from the dominating countries should impress their technique on the native workers, so in this Dutch glass we see the styles of other countries reflected.

Fig. 28. DUTCH GLASS, GOLD DECORATION
Dutch Green Glass Decorated with Gold, 1606. Emblem
of Prince Maurice of Orange.

Fig. 29. ROEMERS
Dutch Green Glass. Left and Centre 16th Century. Right 17th Century.

(See page 74)

Fig. 30.  DIAMOND-EN-
GRAVED ROEMER
Green Glass,  Dutch Diamond
Engraving, 17th Century.

*(See pages* 74 *and* 75)

Fig. 31.  ENGRAVED BOTTLE
Green Dutch Bottle.  Diamond Engraving, 1684.

Fig. 32.  TALL DRINKING
GLASS
Dutch Glass, Facon de Venise,
with Portrait of Prince Frederick Hendrik of Orange (1625-
47).  Diamond Engraving.

(*See page* 76)

Fig. 33.  DRINKING GLASS
Dutch Glass with Diamond En-
graving.  Second Half of 17th
Century.

[ 65 ]

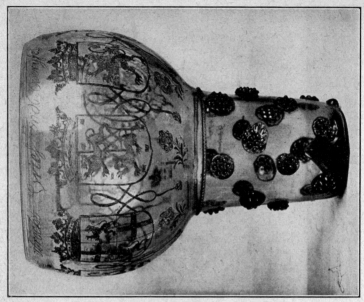

Fig. 34-A. ENGRAVED GLASS, GOLD
DECORATION

Fig. 34-B. ENGRAVED GLASS, GOLD DECORATION

Green Roemer of 1650 with Heraldry in Diamond
Engraving of Orange, Spain and the Provinces
of the Netherlands.

Fig. 35.   COVERED BIRTH CUP
Colourless  English  Crystal  Glass.
Dutch  Cutting,  18th  Century.

Fig. 36.   GERMAN GLASS
BEAKER
Enamelled Glass Dated 1687.

(*See pages* 77 *and* 79)

Fig. 37. COVERED CUP

(*See page 80*)

Fig. 38. "WILLKOMMEN" GLASSES
Fig. 39. HUNTING GLASSES

(*See pages* 81 *and* 82)

[ 69 ]

Fig. 40.   GERMAN GLASSES

(*See page* 83)

The earliest record of Flemish glass is an item in the inventory of Charles V of France, dated 1380: "A goblet of white Flemish glass mounted in silver." In 1421 a certain Annieul was a glass-maker at Namur. By 1503 there existed in Flanders a manufactory of glass mirrors, and in that year the Venetian Council authorized Andrea and Domenico Gallo to make mirrors in Flanders with the Flemish firm.*

The inventory of Marguerite of Austria made in 1523 mentions "a large green drinking glass with cover and foot of silver gilt." No doubt Marguerite of Austria's glass was similar to the one shown in Figure 24. They were sometimes called "beherscrew" and this glass is also green and has a mounting of silver-gilt. It belongs to the City of Amsterdam, and is on exhibition at the Rijks Museum, Amsterdam. The story of the travels of the Venetian glass-makers all over Europe where they either established glass-works or worked in those already established makes an important item in the story of glass-making in the Low Countries.

The great Flemish family of De Colnet were associated with the Ferros from Venice and worked at making glass in the Venetian manner. Antwerp, Brussels and Liége became the great headquarters after the sixteenth century, and made glass successfully for over two hundred years.†

*The Expert, 1908.
† Hartshorne: "English Glasses."
Figure 24, page 45.

The important privileges accorded to the Venetian glass-workers in Flanders only applied to those who worked in glass made in Venetian style, which was also allowed to be imported. Figure 25 shows a beautiful "mill beker" latticinio glass and silver, made during the seventeenth century, and belonging to the Rijks Museum. Such pieces as this and the one previously shown were chiefly used as ornaments on the richly carved and inlaid cupboards of the period, and of which every well-to-do Dutch family boasted one or two.

Soon after 1713 Brussels ceased to make glass in Venetian style. A series of letters by M. Schuermans, entitled, "Muranese and Altarist Glass Workers," throws much light on the Italian workers in The Netherlands. Besides the Venetian glass which was legally imported and that which was made by duly licensed Italian glass-workers in Antwerp and other cities, there was much glass in Venetian style illegally made over the French border, or in Germany, at the beginning of the seventeenth century.

A glass factory was founded in Brussels in 1626 by Antonio Miotti who made "glasses, vases, and cups of fine crystal glass and of all colours." By 1658 the names of the foreign glass-makers almost wholly disappear and those of a long line of distinguished Flemish master glass-blowers appear. Among them were H. and

*Figure 25, page 45.*

L. Bonhomme, T. Lambotte, Barbe de Thiers and A. Duquesne.*

The Bonhommes were progressive business men, and by the end of the seventeenth century had contrived to get control of the glassware trade in Belgium and even as far as Verdun. Of this period there are occasionally to be found some very charming Flemish glasses of a thin glass, without stems, and in a variety of colours, dark amber, red, pale green, pale blue and russet brown. Both Liége and Brussels claim their invention.

The next step was to mount the bowl on a stem with one or more bulbs, and with a domed and folded foot. During the seventeenth and eighteenth centuries the Dutch carried the art of scratching or engraving on glass with a diamond point to a high point of perfection. Figure 26 shows two very ornamental glasses of the seventeenth century with diamond-point engraving. The taller one is the property of the Koninblijk Oudheidkundig Genootschap, and both are displayed at the Rijks Museum.

Ladies considered this diamond-scratched work an elegant accomplishment, and several became noted for the excellence of their work. The daughters of Roemer Vischer were very skillful and justly celebrated, and a dark green roemer engraved by Anna Roemer, 1646, is the central piece in Figure 27. The taller glass decorated with the heraldic device of Schoonhoven,

* *The Expert.*
*Figures 26 and 27, page 46.*

1663, is the property of the Koninblijk Oudheidkundig
Genootschap, and all are at the Rijks Museum. These
roemers, beloved of the Dutch glass-makers, were made
in great variety. They bear a close resemblance to
German glasses of the same period. The color is green,
the shape somewhat clumsy, and the decoration, glass
threads drawn over the surface, or nuppen or prunts
applied to the stems. These prunts were in different
designs. Some of them were sharp and pointed when
the glass was dropped hot upon the stem, as in Figure
28. Rather uncomfortable to hold, one would think.
This roemer, decorated with gold with the emblem of
Prince Maurice of Orange, is green glass and is dated
1606. It is at the Rijks Museum.

Sometimes the prunts are very decorative, softly
rounded, like the tallest one in Figure 29, which is
painted with allegories of Peace and Liberty, in brown-
black enamel. The other two are early types, belonging to the sixteenth century. The glass in these roemers
varied from a pale greenish tint to one so dark as to be
almost black. The prunts might be lighter, darker or
the same shade.

The typical roemer consists of three parts, the cup
or bowl, the hollow stem with prunts, and a foot, also
hollow, made of a thread of glass coiled round and
round. A very graceful one of the seventeenth century, with beautiful diamond-point etching, ascribed
to Maria Fesselschade is shown in Figure 30. Not only

*Figures 28, 29 and 30, pages 63 and 64.*

to drinking glasses was this free and flowing style of diamond-point engraving applied. A fine dark green bottle is shown in Figure 31, dated 1684, and engraved by Willem van Heemskirk. The green glass of some of these pieces is a wonderful shade, and shows off the engraving to great advantage.

The glasses made in the Prince Bishopric of Liége after 1725 are very interesting to collectors, and an immense number of them were made. In *The Expert,* an English magazine, for the year 1908, a classification of these glasses is given and follows here:

*"One.* The oldest are very graceful in shape, engraved on the rims are arabesques. They have stems with delicate bulbs half way up, with tears in them.

*"Two.* These have long slender bowls set on short stems, with moulded tops and bases.

*"Three.* Wedding glasses, fine in shape and colour and always sapphire blue.

*"Four.* Small pieces, with furrowed or fluted bowls, the stem being drawn out of the bowl, with plain folded feet.

*"Five.* Drinking glasses with short wide bowls, the stems with a series of bulbs, and foot always folded.

*"Six.* Openwork glass baskets with trailed and pinched bases.

*"Seven.* Holy-water stoups decorated with blue and white twisted rods.

*"Eight.* Burgundy glasses, covered with small round

*Figure 31, page 64.*

spots in relief, with moulded stems and domed and folded feet.

"*Nine.* Small cups in the form of cavalry boots, sometimes edged and spurred with blue.

"*Ten.* Long-necked spa water bottles, shaped like flattened gourds, with painted wooden stands."

Figure 32 shows a very elegant tall drinking glass in Venetian style, with portrait style of decoration in diamond-point etching which was so popular a feature. This portrait is of Prince Frederick Hendrik of Orange (1625-47), and the glass is at the Rijks Museum. The exquisite delicacy of the diamond-point work shows to great advantage in this specimen, the portrait being exceptionally clear, as are the bird and vine which almost cover the rest of the surface.

The men who did this class of work were artists, not mere mechanical workmen. Gerard Dou, Rembrandt's celebrated pupil, was the son of a glass-worker, and served an apprenticeship to a man named Dolendo, an etcher on glass, before he began to paint.

The process of stippling or using minute dots to form a pattern was another Dutch method of decoration. The result is a very delicate and beautiful pattern hardly more than a mere hoar frost upon the glass. This method is said to have been invented by Frans Greenwood, born at Rotterdam, 1680, and whose last work was dated 1743.* Figure 33 shows a fine example

* Dillon: "Glass."
*Figures 32 and 33, page 65.*

of this work, and belongs to the second half of the seventeenth century. It is at the Rijks Museum.

Another artist famed in this style of work was Aart Schouman, and also a man named Wolf, of whom little is known except that he married in 1787 and died in 1808.

Two interesting prunted drinking glasses, elaborately engraved, are shown in Figure 34. The one with the thorny foot belongs to Koninblijk Oudheidkundig Genootschap, Amsterdam, and is engraved with the heraldic devices of Orange, Spain and the Provinces of The Netherlands. It is dated 1650. The other, marked "Utrecht," with elaborate heraldic devices on it in gold, belongs to the Pennsylvania Museum, and is of probably the same period.

From the middle of the seventeenth century Antwerp made very beautiful glasses with covers. During the seventeenth and eighteenth centuries, engraved glass in Bohemian style was made in Flanders, but was less choice than the contemporary engraved glass found in Holland.

Much glass made in England in the early eighteenth century was sent to Flanders to be engraved. An example is shown in Figure 35, a birth cup, English glass, engraved in Bohemian style in Flanders. At the present time much Flanders glass is sent to this country for engraving, and sold here. A curious change from the old method.

*Figures 34 and 35, pages 66 and 67.*

THE earliest records of glass-making in Germany come from the neighbourhood of Cologne during the Roman period. Although there are specimens of this early glass in the Cologne Museum and a native industry developed after the fall of the Roman power, full recorded details do not begin much before the sixteenth century. It is known that a guild of glass-makers existed at Nuremberg as early as 1373. Among other objects, small convex mirrors were made in large quantities in southern Germany and continued to be made till comparatively recent times. They were known as "bull's eyes." Small globes of glass were blown and while they were still hot they were passed through a mixture of tin, antimony and tar. When the globe was entirely coated with the metallic compound and sufficiently cooled, it was cut into convex lenses, which reflected small but clear images.

The map of Europe has changed so constantly during the last few hundred years that the boundaries of countries are no longer the same. For example, the Germans claim that the potash-lime glass which lent itself so readily to cut and engraved decoration, and was so clear and colourless, was their invention, although it is always known as Bohemian glass.

But it is a fact that most of the early glass, the six-teenth century product, and perhaps even earlier, had a close resemblance, no matter whether it was made in Germany, Holland or the Low Countries. The colour of the glass was green as a rule, and the decoration was glass studs or prunts, sometimes varied with threads of glass applied in various ways.

Glass furnaces were established in Vienna in 1428. In 1531 the town council of Nuremberg offered a sub-sidy to attract workmen from Murano. But although the German glass-workers were instructed by men from Venice, the Italian influence hardly prevailed over the coarser German taste.*

The vessels made were chiefly drinking glasses of one form or another, and the early form of decoration was enamelling in high colours. These capacious tall drinking glasses, decorated with portraits of German emperors, the imperial eagle, arms of the states, battle scenes and other vainglorious devices, became im-mensely popular. The glass shown in Figure 36 is a beaker with the arms of Duke Johann Georg III of Saxony, dated 1687 and inscribed "Hoff Kellerey Dres-den." It is at the Victoria and Albert Museum.

The earliest known of these enamelled glasses is dated 1553, and the demand for them lasted till well into the eighteenth century.†

The glasses known as "roemers" were perhaps the

* Dillon: "Glass."
† Wylde: "German Enamelled Glasses."
*Figure 36, page 67.*

most popular shape of all. The "igel" was a squat tumbler covered with prunts. The "passglas," another popular drinking glass, something like the modern loving cup, was marked with horizontal lines or rings at regular intervals, to show the amount of liquor to be taken at a draught. It can hardly be imagined that one of these portentous drinkers took less than his allotted amount.

At first the roemer was but a tumbler with a foot formed by a ring of glass wound around its base. But gradually it acquired a waist covered with prunts, and later a foot and in some instances a cover, so that finally it became a rather dignified looking object, like the one seen in Figure 37. This very beautiful specimen is at the Pennsylvania Museum, Philadelphia.

The oldest method of painting glass in Germany was by use of oil paints combined with engraving. Oil of lavender was the medium used, and then the whole decoration was lacquered over. Of course this method proved most unsatisfactory, for the decoration chipped off very easily and left only spots of colour.

The enamelled glasses known as Fichtelberger glasses were produced at the glass-works in the Fichtel mountains, northeast of Bavaria. C. H. Wylde in an article in *The Connoisseur* on "German Glass Drinking Vessels Painted in Enamel Colours," says that probably the Bischofsgrun Kiln in this range of moun-

*Figure 37, page 68.*

tains was the first in Germany to produce enamelled glasses.

The cylinder shape of glass which was the most common and popular form of glass used in the sixteenth and seventeenth centuries, lent itself readily to decoration. The huge glass known as "Willkommen" would seem large enough to floor the heartiest drinker. These were originally used by a host to welcome his newly arrived guest, a welcome cup. Sometimes they had a pointed base and could not be set down till emptied. Mr. Wylde declares that the term "Wiederkom" by which these glasses are known in England is a misnomer, Willkommen being the proper term. Three fine examples of these glasses are shown in Figure 38; they are all in the Victoria and Albert Museum.

The centre glass with cover is the type known as "Reichshumpen" or "Adlerglas," so called from the decoration of the double-headed eagle of the Holy Roman Empire with the armorial shields of fifty-six various kingdoms, states, and towns of the dominion. Above is the inscription, "Das Helig Romish Reich mit Sampt Seinen Gliedern." On the reverse side is the date. An example of one of these Adlergläser which is at the British Museum has a crucifix painted on the breast of the eagle.

The smaller of the other two glasses shows the portrait of a miner and his wife, with armorial device showing a pick and hammer and a miner's lamp. This

Figure 38, page 69.

glass is dated 1671. One may be pardoned for wondering if it was the property of a coal miner. The third glass is more understandable. It was made for a coopers' guild. These guilds were rich and powerful organizations, and at their halls had rich silver cups as well as glass. On this glass is painted twelve scenes of the craft, showing the various stages in the construction of a barrel, from cutting the timber in the forest to the completed cask in the cellar, from which the cooper is quenching his thirst.

There are found, occasionally, glasses painted in brown monochrome. These are called "Schapergläser" from the name of the artist, Johann Schaper. He was the most distinguished of all painters of glass vessels. He was born at Harburg near Hamburg, and lived at Nuremberg from 1640 to 1670, when he died.

The two glasses in Figure 39 are called hunting glasses. They date from the eighteenth century. The walls of the glasses are double, and between them are placed gold and silver foil over which the decoration is painted. Hunting scenes were used and the outer glass wall was cut in facets, so that the glass was less liable to slip through the fingers. The bases are of ruby glass, and just above is a pattern painted in gold. They were very handsome and decorative glasses.

It is a sidelight on the manners and customs of the times to see that drinking glasses of all descriptions were arranged for the convenience of the heavy drinker.

Figure 39, page 69.

Tumblers had wide bases and roughened sides, goblets had prunts or knops, decanters were many ringed so that they were made as safe as possible for the uncertain fingers of the drinker.

Figure 40 shows a group of interesting glasses belonging to the eighteenth and early nineteenth centuries. They show how closely the German and Bohemian glasses resembled each other. There are the graceful pokale or covered cups, decorated with cutting and engraving. The one on the top row with step cutting on its knopped stem is unusually fine in its proportions. The bottle with handle and pewter lid on the same row is also interesting, the smallness of the objects in the picture failing to show the excellence of the engraving.

The double cruet belongs to the early nineteenth century, and is an agreeable object to look upon, but must have been very difficult to manipulate successfully when filled with vinegar and oil. These pieces are all owned by the Pennsylvania Museum, Philadelphia.

A peculiarly beautiful glass, etched in the manner which was so esteemed in Germany, is shown in Figure 41. It is a covered cup engraved and etched with dancing amorini holding grape-vines loaded with grapes. The knob of the cover is metal enamelled with colour, and on the interior button is enamelled the arms of an archbishop of Treves, with the inscription, "Joan,

*Figures 40 and 41, pages 70 and 87.*

Hugo. D. G. Arc. Trev. PR. EL. EP. SP." It is of the early eighteenth century, and belongs to the Victoria and Albert Museum, London. The height including cover is six and three-quarters inches. This, too, is cut and facetted for safe holding.

IT is only recently that the collector has turned his attention to the interesting and often beautiful glass which has been made in Spain. The very decorative pottery and the rarer porcelain has been ferretted out in every province, but the collector still has a hunting chance when it comes to glass.

Of course the earliest glass, for there were glassworks in Spain as early as the thirteenth century, was frankly an imitation of the famous Venetian glass. No doubt many specimens called Venetian were made at the prosperous factories at Barcelona and Cadalso, where very beautiful pieces were manufactured. The lamp shown in Figure 42 is in Venetian style of the seventeenth century. It is pale amber, the stem supporting a cup for oil, and having two spouts. It belongs to the Victoria and Albert Museum, London, which is peculiarly rich in collections of Spanish glass, from which all the illustrations of Spanish glass used here are taken.

An interesting decoration on glass which has been attributed to Venice has now been proved by records to have been made in the Spanish peninsula. It is enamelling, the prevailing shade being a beautiful apple-green, which sometimes fades into yellow. A

*Figure 42, page 88.*

cup of clear glass is shown in Figure 43 with enamel decoration. The leaping deer which was such a favourite theme with glass-makers of all countries is shown here chased by hounds. The centre ornament is a flying bird. This piece is of the sixteenth century.

In the early records of Spanish glass-making, particular mention is made of two kinds of glass, vidrio, and vidrio cristalino. The latter was a pure white glass more like rock-crystal, and the former was just common glass.

Señor Juan F. Riano, who is an authority on Spanish objects of art, says in a pamphlet on the subject written for the Victoria and Albert Museum, that Al Makari, an Arabian author quoting from another Arabian author, this latter of the thirteenth century, states that "Almeria was also famous for the fabrication of all sorts of vases and utensils, whether of iron, copper or glass."

Yet it appears that glass must have been made in Spain even earlier than that, for in the Victoria and Albert Museum there is a large collection of goldsmiths' work, and in it is a portion of a necklace made of different coloured glass beads, with five beads of gilt metal. This fragment was found in an earthen pot in Murcia, and belongs to the latter half of the eleventh century. Many jewels of silver or silver-gilt set with glass stones and dating from the sixteenth century are

Figure 43, page 89.

Fig. 41.  COVERED CUP, ETCHED AND ENGRAVED
German.   Early 18th Century.

(*See page* 83)

[ 87 ]

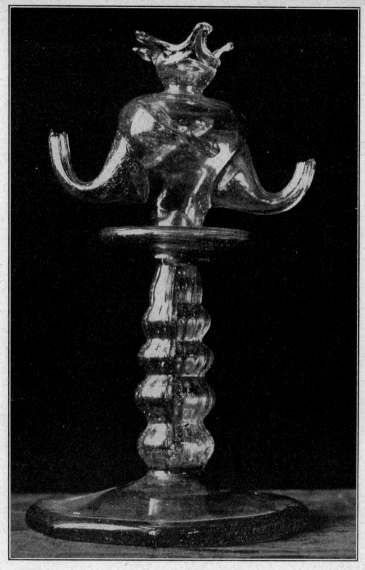

Fig. 42. SPANISH LAMP
Pale Amber Glass in the Form of a Candlestick, Supporting a Reservoir
with Two Spouts and Serrated Ornament. Spanish. Cartagena
17th Century.

(*See page* 85)

Fig. 43.  TAZZA, ENAMELLED
Clear Glass Painted in Enamel Colours.  Spanish.  16th Century.

(*See page* 86)

Fig. 44. JUG, MOTTLED GLASS
Blue and White Mottled Glass. Spanish. Cadalso. 17th Century.
(*See page* 96)

Fig. 45. COVERED BOWL AND TRAY
Plain Glass with Bouquets and Serrated Borders in Gold. 18th Century, Spanish.
(See page 96)

Fig. 46. GLASS BOWL, ENGRAVED
Plain Glass, Oval Bowl with Lip, Engraved with a Château and
Trees. Winged Handle Ending in a Shell. Spanish. 18th Century.
San Ildefonso.

(*See page* 97)

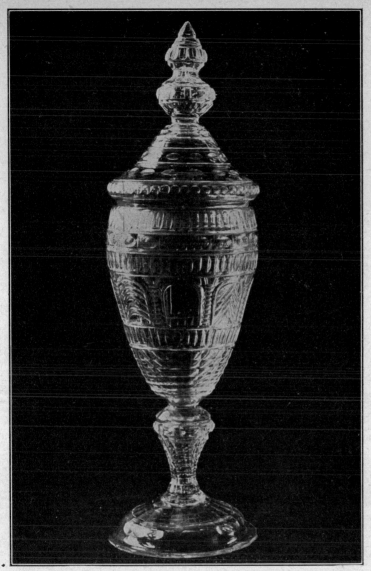

Fig. 47. COVERED CUP, WITH CUTTING
Standing Glass with Cover. Plain Glass Richly Cut. Spanish, San
Ildefonso. 18th Century.

(*See page* 97)

Fig. 48.  GOBLET, CUT AND ENGRAVED
Plain Glass, Cut and Engraved.  Spanish.  San Ildefonso.
18th Century.

(*See page* 97)

also to be seen in the Victoria and Albert Museum collections.

Barcelona, one of the towns which belonged to the Christians in Spain, was early a notable centre for the excellence and beauty of its glass. In 1324 a special municipal edict forbade the erection of ovens for glass-making within the city on account of the danger from fire, to the rest of the population.

Queen Isabel, beloved of every good American, in 1475 granted to the monks of the convent of San Geronimo de Guisando the privilege of erecting a glass furnace at Venta de los Toros de Guisando, with tax exemption from all sales. In 1503 Ferdinand of Aragon sent to Queen Isabel 274 pieces of Barcelona glass.*

In 1455 permission was granted to the glass-makers to form a corporation under the patronage of Saint Bernardino. This corporation was similar in purpose to the guilds of other countries. Few of the rules and regulations governing it are known, but in 1779 in an account of the industries of Barcelona, Capmany writes that a master glass-maker had to serve an apprenticeship of six years.

During the fifteenth, sixteenth, and seventeenth centuries, choice glass was made at Barcelona and in sufficient quantities so that it could be exported. Geronimo Paulo writes in 1491 about the remarkable things made at Barcelona. He says, "They also send to Rome

* Schuerman's Letters.

and other places many glass vessels of different sorts and kinds, which may well compete with those of Venice."

In 1780, Mataro, Cervallo, and Almatret, three towns of Cataluña, were all making glass. At Cadalso in the province of Toledo enough glass was made at the beginning of the sixteenth century, according to a contemporary writer, "to furnish the whole kingdom." But the industry failed, and by 1750 glass was no longer made there. Figure 44 shows an interesting jug made at Cadalso in the seventeenth century. It is mottled blue and white with blue rims, and is most attractive. Some glass was made at Toledo, for there are records of what was furnished, principally lamps, to the cathedral.

A price list was issued in 1680 settling the prices at which glass made at Barcelona, Valdemaqueda and Villafranca should be sold at Madrid. The glass-works at La Granja de San Ildefonso were opened in 1725, and they produced very beautiful pieces, chiefly white glass decorated with engraving, cutting and gilding. Permanent gilding fixed with heat is said to be the invention of a Spaniard, Don Sigismondo Brun, and an example of this work is shown in Figure 45, a bowl with cover and tray. It is plain glass and all the decoration is in gold; it dates from the eighteenth century.

The glass of southern Spain shows the influence of the East. This is seen particularly in the products of

*Figures 44 and 45, pages 90 and 91.*

the provinces of Granada, Andalusia, Murcia and Almeria. Italian glass was taken as a model at Catalonia, Mataro, Almatret and Cervallo. Also in the interior the Italian workmen, greatest travellers ever, notwithstanding the drastic rules forbidding them to leave Italy, set the style for the native workers to follow. Cadalso, Recuenco, Cebreros, Valdemaqueda and San Martin de Valdeiglesias all followed Venetian models.*

La Granja de San Ildefonso made glass in Bohemian style. They made jars, vases, bottles and other hollow ware, profusely decorated with spines, ridges, button work and threads. Some of this glass is shown in Figures 46 and 47. In the first example the glass is clear and the decoration engraving, trees and landscape. The winged handle decorated with spines ends in a shell which is attached to the bowl. Figure 47 shows that the glass made at San Ildefonso could compare favourably with the glass made at other European centres. The shape of the covered jug is most pleasing, and the cutting attractive. Both these pieces are of the eighteenth century.

In Figure 48 is shown an important piece of engraved and cut glass. This goblet, with its heavily knopped stem and engraving and cutting of a higher order, is made from the clear glass which the Spanish

* Dillon: "Glass."
*Figures 46, 47 and 48, pages 92, 93 and 94.*

called vidrio cristalino, and it was no wonder that other nations were glad to claim it as their own.

Almeria was the most important town for the making of Spanish glass of Moorish type. They made bottles and flasks of odd and often graceful shapes till quite recently.

A glass vessel such as that shown in Figure 49 is used for drinking wine, which seems as characteristic of Spain as the straw-covered wine bottles seem of Italy. The Spanish bottle is made of plain glass with latticinio threads about the neck, which has a trefoil mouth. This particular bottle was made in the eighteenth century, and they were and are still made by many Spanish glass-works. I have had them offered me for sale in different shops in this country which deal in Spanish goods. The modern bottles are of a greenish cast, the glass itself very grainy, and only rarely do they show the latticinio threads about the neck. They are not so easy to drink out of as it might seem, and it has ever been a problem in my mind whether the spout or the lip were the more convenient place from which to sip the contents.

*Figure 49, page III.*

## FRENCH GLASS

OWING to their many improvements in the making of glass, and to the fact that they were so early in the field as notable workers in glass, it is impossible to omit reference to the work of the French, even though so few pieces are likely to come into the hands of the collector. From the sixth century they had dishes of glass for table use, as they are mentioned in a letter from Fortunatus, bishop of Poitiers, to Queen Radegonde, wife of Clotaire I.*

In 1338 a document was drawn up by Humbert, Dauphin of Viennois, setting down the privileges to be granted to a glass-maker named Guionet, who was to work on the land of the Dauphin. It also sets down what Guionet was to pay for this privilege. This list is given by M. Sauzay in his book, "Wonders of Glass Making."

"The Dauphin resigns to Guionet a part of the forest of Chambarant, in order that he may establish a glass manufactory there on condition that the latter supply annually for his house one hundred dozen glasses in the form of bells, twelve dozen small glasses with wide tops, twenty dozen goblets or cups with feet, twelve amphorae, thirty-six dozen chamber utensils, twelve

* "Wonders of Glass Making."

[ 99 ]

large porringers, six dishes, six dishes without edges, twelve pots, twelve ewers, five small vessels called gottefles, one dozen salt cellars, twenty dozen lamps, six dozen chandeliers, one dozen large cups, one dozen small barrels, and lastly six large casks for carrying wine." This made a total of two thousand four hundred and thirty-five objects, annually. Quite a price to pay for his "privileges."

As early as 677 A.D. many Greek workmen were called to France, and Normandy was the first country to grant special privileges to glass-workers. In the tenth and eleventh centuries several noble families received special privileges as glass-makers and these were confirmed by successive sovereigns till the eighteenth century. The Crusaders brought home many improvements in methods of glass-making. Charles V gave all glass-makers exemption from taxes.

That romantic figure, King Réne of Anjou, when he lost the throne of Naples retired to Provence where he busied himself with glass-making (1409-80). Dauphiné, Languedoc, Lyonnaise, Poitou, Nivernais, were all early in the field in establishing glass-houses. From the fourteenth century till the present day Nivernais has made glass, though the later product was principally bottles. Paris herself, Loraine and Picardy all made glass before the seventeenth century. French glass of a period as late as the sixteenth century is rarely seen even in Museums. There are two or three specimens in the British Museum, tall large glasses with painted or enamelled decoration of figures and mottoes on them. These large glasses were known as flûtes, the word flûtes still being a familiar French expression for hard drinking. The Hotel Cluny also has a few pieces, but although there were quantities of glass made all over France, there is no gathering anywhere that can properly be called a collection.

Figure 50 shows a bottle with the enamelled decoration already mentioned, consisting of a coat of arms and the inscription "Damoiselle Marie Françoise Therese Pobertine Malatov de la Mairie, 1726." The glass is clear, of the quality made in all countries at that period, and the screw top is of pewter. This illustration, as well as the others used to illustrate French glass, was taken from glass at the Metropolitan Museum of Art, New York.

Another piece of probably the same period is the beaker shown in Figure 51. This is of clear glass decorated with enamel and gold, bearing the inscription, which does not show in the illustration, but which fills the space between the two upper rows of dots, "Gentil Div Te Parvoye." One of the most interesting things about this beaker is the high domed foot with folded rim. The rim is folded over on top in English fashion rather than in Venetian style, in which case the rim would have been folded over and under.

In 1665 a mirror factory was opened in the Faubourg

*Figures 50 and 51, page 112.*

St. Antoine, Paris, where specially imported workmen from Venice taught French workmen how to make mirrors. In order to make the homemade product fashionable, in 1672 Louis XIV had them set in his coach and in a gallery at Versailles which has always been known as the "Gallerie des Glaces." In this historic gallery have been enacted many of the great moments of France, some of them as recent as the late war.

It was Richard Lucas de Nehou who founded this factory in 1665, and he called it "Manufactoire Royale des Glaces." The elder de Nehou died in 1675, and it seems as if when he had learned what the Venetians had to teach, he let them go and set about making improvements on their methods. His son Louis in 1688 invented the method of casting glass plates which allows the manufacture of glasses of almost unlimited size. The glass-houses were moved from Paris to St. Gobain in 1693 where they have been in operation ever since.

The early method of plating looking-glasses was tedious and difficult, but in 1855 a new method was invented by a Frenchman, M. Petitjean, and now most modern mirrors are made by depositing on the glass a coating of silver.

Many privileges were granted to the first de Nehou. He was allowed to "take as co-partners even nobles and ecclesiastics without it being derogatory to their nobility." * In fact the gentlemen glass-makers were relieved of all imposts, which were considerable at the time. These gentlemen glass-workers had begun to make glass in the Middle Ages. There are quantities of glass fragments to be found in many parts of Poitiers, and the names of such towns as Vieille, Verrières, Voirie, Verrines, come from their glass-works. Fully thousands of parts of vases and other fragments have been found at Terre-Noire, Bordeaux.

A very graceful and beautiful vase of clear glass is shown in Figure 52. It perhaps leans to the Venetian style in its manner of decoration, for it has a thread of blue glass about its lip and neck and also a blue rim. The interlaced crescents and the double D are in blue also, and are the insignia of Diane de Poitiers, who was notable for the works of art with which she surrounded herself. Any one who has seen that charming château of Chenonceau which she arranged to suit her fancy and built across the river Cher, would not doubt for a moment that such a delightful object as this vase would have fitted admirably with her belongings, and in her favourite colour, blue. The period of this vase is possibly as early as the sixteenth century.

The Imperial factory of Frontincennes, at Forêt-Eu, cradle of all Norman glass-works, is supposed to have been founded in the second century and is claimed by the French to be the oldest in the world. The glass-

* "Wonders of Glass Making."
*Figure 52, page 112.*

house of Vonêche, near Givet, was founded about 1800 by M. d'Artigues. By the treaty of 1815, it became outside French territory and was transferred to the Low Countries. But d'Artigues obtained the right of sending his glass duty free for three years into France, on the condition of founding crystal glass works in France during the interval. This he did by buying the glasshouse of St. Anne at Baccarat, where up to that time only common glass had been produced, and establishing crystal glass works which have become the most important of their kind in France.*

Not only crystal glass of a wonderful clearness and beauty was and is made at Baccarat, but they made what they called "coloured crystals" as well. These coloured glasses were sent to foreign countries to compete with Bohemian glass wares, which, M. Sauzay claims, "are less finished in detail than ours; the defective objects are put up for sale with the others; the mouths of bottles and other like objects are made with a carelessness which would not be tolerated in France."

Owing to her large business in wines and liquors France has made great quantities of bottles. The first glass bottle factory in France is said to have been established at Quicangrogne in 1290.†

The Robinet pump was the invention of a Frenchman, and greatly facilitates the manufacture of bottles.

* Hartshorne: "Old English Glasses."
† Sauzay: "Wonders of Glass Making."

Besides the strictly utilitarian bottles there were many very beautiful bottles, decanters and jugs made at Clichy-la-Garenne. These rivalled in shape and elegance the best of the Venetian glasses from which they were modelled, and some were very beautifully cut and engraved. A bottle showing the Venetian influence is shown in Figure 53. This bottle is of clear glass with crimped straps applied to the sides, and medallions of fleurs-de-lis applied to the front and reverse. The neck has quite an elaborate collar and the body has a hole through the centre. Sometimes they were called "pilgrim bottles," and are found much less ornamental than this one but still with the hole in the centre. They were also made of coloured glass, generally of shades of transparent blue or green.

Figure 54 shows another style of bottle, of the splashed decoration which was made not only on the Continent, but in England as well. The example shown has handles and crimped straps of clear glass, and is interesting as showing how general was this splashing and striping among glass-workers. The wine glass shown in Figure 55 has a French coin of silver, bearing the date 1727, blown in the knop in its stem. The rings above and below the knop and the folded foot all point to the work of that period. It is not always possible to date the specimens by the date of the coin, but in this case they coincide. There is a chain-like decoration on the bowl of the glass, and raised work in dia-

*Figures 53, 54 and 55, pages 112 and 113.*

mond shape below it. The method of superimposing a layer of glass on the original body to form a decoration is shown in the graceful jug of clear glass given in Figure 56. On the foot are placed three medallions showing fleurs-de-lis, the nearest the French with their graceful fancies could come to the use of prunts so popular with the Germans and Dutch, and as a general rule so clumsy. This decoration from French hands makes them almost as effective as a coat-of-arms.

The Bohemian style of ornamentation was often heavy and consisted of castles, men and women, sheep and other animals. The French on the other hand used only floral designs remarkable for their elegance and beauty. The idea was generally prevalent that Bohemia alone held the secret for the manufacture of glass of those wonderful shades of red, blue, green and yellow which have so long been called by its name. But in 1837 a meeting was called in France, encouraged by M. Dumas and the "Société d'Encouragement," at which a prize was offered for the most beautiful coloured glass. Glass-makers of all nations competed and the prizes were won by two Frenchmen, M.M. Fontenay and Bontemps.

Another field in which France excelled, although it is of comparatively recent date, is the making of artificial gems and pearls.

More interesting to the collector are the very beautiful paper-weights, called millefiori, which were origi-

Figure 56, page 113.

nated in Venice, later made in Bohemia, but perfected in France. There are many collections of these interesting objects in this country, and it is difficult to decide the nationality of each specimen. But as a rule the finest ones, made of a myriad of delicately coloured florets, are French. The glass which surrounds the florets is clearer and less bubbly than the Venetian and the patterns are smaller than the Bohemian. England, particularly Bristol, also made these weights in many styles and America took a hand and manufactured these pretty trifles. These will be spoken of in their proper places.

TO the collector of old glass, only the examples of table glass or pieces for domestic use appeal particularly. But to the inhabitants of those countries which were struggling after the Middle Ages to improve the character of their dwellings, and increase their comforts, window glass, even thick and poor in colour, was of vast importance.

In 675 A.D. the Abbot of Wearmouth, Benedict Biscop, sent to France for artisans to make glass. But it was not till 1350 A.D. that enough flat colourless glass was supplied by a glass-maker of Chiddingfold to glaze the windows in St. George's chapel, Windsor, and the chapel of St. Stephen, Westminster.*

Looking-glasses and drinking glasses were next in importance, many of these being imported from Venice. George Gascoigne wrote in 1572 the first regular verse satire, and he called it "Steel Glass." In it he bewailed the folly of the age which could no longer be content with a good glass of steel nor yet one of common glass. But now, he says, every wight must have

"The christal glass which glimseth brave and bright,
And shews the thing much better far than it."

By 1615 all previous patents for making glass with wood had been revoked, and a new patent issued for

* Dillon: "Glass."

using coal. From this time on the covered crucible was used to protect the metal from the gas and smoke of burning coal. And, by the way, the trust is not so recent a business factor as one might think. In 1617 Sir R. Mansel, vice-admiral and treasurer of the Navy, acquired the sole rights for making glass in England, and he held on to it for thirty years.

Quantities of these small mirrors were made in every glass-making country, and were universally worn. In the play the "City Madam," by Massinger, written about 1624, these mirrors are referred to.

"Enter Lady Frugal, Anne, Mary and Millicent in several postures with looking-glasses at their girdles."

In "Cynthia's Revels," one of the characters says:

"Where is your page? Call for your casting bottle, and place your mirror in your hat, as I told you."

Thevenot writes in 1663, "The Mogul women are so fond of seeing themselves that they wear a bit of looking-glass an inch in diameter, set instead of a precious stone, in one of their rings."

After the Mansel patent expired, the Duke of Buckingham became a glass-maker. He was not able to secure a monopoly of glass-making in England, but he succeeded in 1663 in having the importation of many kinds of glass prohibited. At his glass-works, according to Evelyn's Diary, in 1677 were made "vases of mettal as cleare, ponderous and thick as chrystal; also looking-glasses far larger and better than any which came from Venice."

By 1696, Houghton in "Letters for the Improvement of Trade and Husbandry," records that eighty-eight glass-houses were working in England. The eighteenth century saw great development in all branches of the glass industry, and in the beauty and character of the glass for domestic use. This was the most important period in the glass industry, for the making of flint glass was perfected, and the art of glass cutting reached its greatest beauty.

It might almost be said that the social history of England was written in her drinking glasses. The precious metals, leather, pottery, porcelain, pewter, glass, have all been called on for the tipster's delight, and undoubtedly the goldsmith and the glass-blower created the objects of greatest beauty. The reason for this is easily seen. The importance of the inn, particularly to those who dared to travel on roads frequented by highwaymen; the public house, the resort of the country yokel; the coffee houses, taverns and clubs where the men about town disported themselves, were far more important than they are now. All these places depended upon the liquid refreshment they were able to offer for their prosperity. It is no wonder, then, that the manufacturer of drinking vessels, for a period of nearly three centuries, found it absolutely

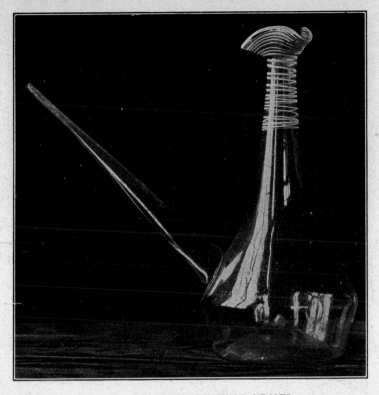

Fig. 49.  SPANISH DRINKING VESSEL
Bottle.  Plain Glass with Long Neck and Trefoil Mouth, Surrounded
by Latticinio Lines, with Long Spout.  Used for Drinking Wine.
18th Century.  Spanish.

(*See page* 98)

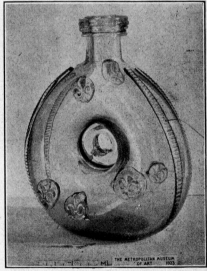

Fig. 50.  FRENCH BOTTLE,
ENAMELLED

Fig. 51.  BEAKER, ENAMELLED

Fig. 52.  FRENCH VASE

Fig. 53.  BOTTLE, CLEAR GLASS

(*See pages* 101, 103 *and* 105)

Fig. 54. BARREL-SHAPED FLASK

Fig. 55. WINE GLASS WITH
COIN IN STEM

Fig. 56. FRENCH JUG, CLEAR
GLASS

(*See pages* 105 *and* 106)

Fig. 57. ENGLISH WINE GLASSES

(*See page* 123)

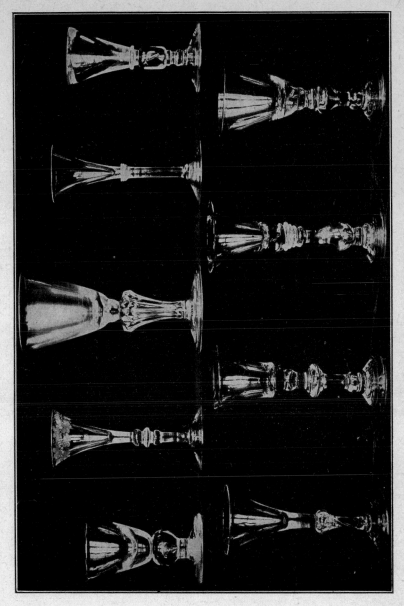

Fig. 58. WINE GLASSES WITH KNOPPED STEMS

(See page 127)

Fig. 59. FOUR GROUPS OF STEMS

(*See page* 128)

Fig. 60. SET OF ENGLISH CUT GLASS

(See page 148)

Fig. 61. SET OF LUSTRES

(See page 149)

necessary to make jugs, mugs, bottles and drinking glasses in enormous quantities.

Turn where you will in English literature, and the only difference in the convivial habits of the highest or the lowest seems to have been the quality of what they consumed. In "Hudibras," by Samuel Butler, published 1663-78, he writes about Fleet Street, London.

> "That tipling street,
> Distinguished by the name of Fleet,
> Where tavern signs hang thicker far
> Than trophies down at Westminster;
> And every bacchanalian landlord
> Displays his ensign or his standard,
> Bidding defiance to each brother,
> As if at wars with one another;
> Their only quarrel being who
> Can with most art and interest brew;
> That is, in short, about who is't
> That can the most deceive his guest,
> Draw the worst wine and thrive the best."

What were known as "tavern glasses" were of course stout glasses which could stand hard wear, and the quality of the glass, though perhaps not its size, advanced as its users progressed in the social scale. Nor were the uses of the glasses solely for drinking. Withers writing about 1650 says:

> "From sudden brawls do sudden stabs arise,
> And sometimes in revenge the quart pot flies,
> Ioyn'd stools and glasses make a rustling rumour."

During the eighteenth century the number of clubs in London seems almost unbelievable, and apparently no one was too poor or too criminal to be deprived of the benefit of belonging to a club where he could meet with others of his kind. "The Secret History of Clubs," written by an eccentric named Ned Ward, who died in 1731, gives a list of great length. He names and gives the meeting-places of such clubs as the "No-Nose" which met at the Dog Tavern in Drury Lane; "The Surly Club," "The Club of Ugly Faces," consisting of those to whom Nature had been unkind. There was the club of "Broken Shopkeepers," "Mock Heroes' Club," "Lady's Lap-dog Club," "Beggars' Club," "Quack's Club," the "Thieves' Club," a "Society of Desperadoes who met daily at the Sign of the Half Moon in Old Bailey," and the "Small Coalman's Music Club," held in a tavern in Clerkenwell.

In addition there were such famous clubs as the "Brothers' Club," to which none were admitted "but men of wit or men of interest." This club had rules drawn up by Dean Swift in 1711. The most famous club of the century was without doubt the "Kitcat Club," although just who founded it is not known. Peg Woffington, known for her beauty and her wit, was long its president. Some of its eminent members were such literary lights as Addison and Congreve, and such dashing blades as the Dukes of Somerset, Richmond, Grafton, Devonshire and Marlborough; the Earls of Dorset and Manchester, and Sir Robert Walpole, father of Horace the great china collector.

They had a bewildering array of beverages to choose from. Withers' Satires, written about 1650, decries the increase of luxury,

"Their drinks are good and stale,
Of perry, cider, mead, methlegin, ale,
Of beer they have abundantly, but then
This must not serve the richer sort of men,
They with all sorts of foreign wines are sped,
Their cellars are oft fraught with white and red,
Be it French, Italian, Spanish, if they crave it,
Nay, Grecian or Canarian, they may have it.
Cate, Pument, Vervage, if they do desire,
Or Romney, Bastard, Caprike, Osey, Tire,
Muscadell, Malmsey, Clary, what they will
Both head and belly each may have their fill."

To fittingly enjoy this array and to gratify their female friends, toasting glasses, each inscribed with some appropriate lines of verse addressed to certain toasts or reigning beauties of that era, were used by members of the Kitcat club at their weekly meetings. The four lovely daughters of the Duke of Marlborough were so honoured. So were the Duchess of Bonton, Lady Carlisle and a long list of others. Much breakage occurred when the toasts were drunk and Madame de Sevigne's Letters relate that after drinking the King's health it was the custom to break the glass. This was in 1675, and persisted long after.

By the middle of the eighteenth century there were dozens of clubs like the famous "Je ne sais quoi club," which numbered among its members the Prince of Wales and the Dukes of York and Clarence. The nobility and gentry were not alone in their rage for clubs. "There was scarcely a public house," says Sydney in his "England in the Eighteenth Century," "in any respectable neighbourhood of the capital which had not its friends' club, its lottery club, its smoking club, its charity club or choir club in the parlour, where the neighbouring shopkeepers regularly spent their evenings, and where they frequently got drunk, and always drank to some excess."

An exhaustive study of English drinking glasses has been made by Albert Hartshorne. He calls his monumental work, "Old English Glasses." This branch of the subject was and is of peculiar interest to the English collector, since there were excellent opportunities for making more or less complete collections of these objects. Many of the drinking glasses had political interest as well, and considerable of England's history was written in a word or line, or even in a rose or thistle engraved on the bowl of a wine glass. The cost of these relics was not excessive, and the years from 1690 to 1810 was the period of their greatest interest and worth.

The Stuart family with its rises and falls, its romantic history and the remarkable personality of its members, has had much glass inscribed to it by its loyal followers. The Jacobites who drank secretly from a glass inscribed with a white rose, to "the king over the water," long cherished their cause. Some of the glasses in addition to an emblem bore verses of Jacobite songs. There were portraits of "Bonnie Prince Charlie," and of the "Old Pretender," and insignia and mottoes. But these glasses, rare enough in England, are practically unknown here, save for a few which have found their way into Museums.

Four of these glasses are shown in Figure 57; they belong to the Victoria and Albert Museum, London. The pair of wine glasses at the ends engraved with a rose and two rosebuds are emblematic of the Old and Young Pretenders, James II and Charles Edward. At the back of the glass is engraved the oak leaf and the word "Fiat," the meaning of which has never been authoritatively settled. The tallest glass is another rose "Pretenders" glass without the word "Fiat." The fourth glass has engraved on it a portrait of Charles Edward, encircled with a laurel wreath. On the other side are roses, a thistle and a star.

Portraits of military and naval heroes were sometimes engraved on choice pieces of English glass. Nelson and his victories were often eulogised. "Wellington Forever" and Admiral Keppel were both honoured. One inscription recorded by Percy Bate in his book on "English Glass" touches us more nearly. It is "De Negoti. Anno 1772." Mr. Bate suggests that this refers to the judgment delivered that year in the case of the slave Somerset, who was liberated by the courts after being arrested as a slave, on the ground

Figure 57, page 114.

that as soon as he stepped on British soil he became a free man. Mr. Bate assigns these glasses to Bristol, a great Quaker centre, and a "port connected by ties of trade with the slave holding provinces of America." It is not unlikely that some member of the Society of Friends had this rummer so engraved to indicate a forward step in the anti-slavery crusade.

Nor was the cheerful toper forgotten, for glasses of a somewhat later date bear such enlivening mottoes as, "Wine does wonders every day," or "Jove decreed the grape should bleed for me," or "Keep it up."

Three glasses have come down from the stately days of "Good Queen Bess." One of them belonged to that canny queen herself. She owned, to be sure, many of the choicest rarities in her kingdom, for if her loving subjects were a trifle slow in giving such treasures to her, she did not hesitate to suggest that the article would make a good New Year's gift. Queen Elizabeth's glass, which is still preserved in its leather case among the royal collections at Windsor Castle, was made by Jacob Verzellini, a Venetian who worked in Crutched Friars, London, for twenty-one years under a patent dated December 15, 1575.

It was probably Verzellini who first used soda-ash made from seaweed and seaside plants, instead of the crude potash made from fern and wood ashes. Verzellini died in 1606, but some years previous to this the works were taken over by Jerome Bowes. These same works continued in operation till 1641. In 1874 excavations in Broad Street on the site of the old works revealed many fragments of glass. Among them were a square scent bottle, part of a wine glass, and the stem of a wine glass showing a spiral thread of white enamel.*

In the British Museum are two other glass objects made by Verzellini, one a silver-mounted tankard and the other a very beautiful goblet covered with wonderfully florid decoration made with a diamond point, and dated 1586. Percy Bate in his book, "English Glass," tells of a fourth example which came to a London auction-room and was accidentally broken.

The use of glass vessels for domestic purposes was very limited till late in the sixteenth century. Workmen came from Venice, and there also were brought over from Normandy and Lorraine many talented and industrious families who had left France on account of religious disturbances. Among them were the famous glass-working families of Hennezel, de Thietry, du Thisac and du Houx, from Lorraine, and de Bongar and de Cacquery from Normandy. In 1567 Thomas and Balthazar de Hennezel settled in Wisborough Green in Sussex, and after some centuries the name was corrupted into Henzy. Du Thisac became Tyzack, de Thietry became Tittery and de Cacquery, Cockery,

* Dillon: "Glass."

and thus were inscribed in parish registers and other town documents.

Other Lorraine gentlemen glass-makers with their wives and families settled in the copses and spinneys of Petworth, Kirkford, Alfold and other Surrey and Sussex hamlets, where raw material, wood, sand and bracken lay close and handy by, and where they could conceal the mystery of their craft, and from which seclusion they could refuse to mix with the yeomen and common folk who dwelt near by.*

During the sixteenth century small glass furnaces were established in Kent as well as parts of Sussex and Surrey. The workers were nomads ever driven further afield in the search of fuel for their furnaces. Their progress may be traced by broken-down furnaces and cullet heaps, through many English counties and finally into Scotland and Ireland.

Glass-cutting works were operated at Bristol, Birmingham, Belfast, Cork, Dublin, London, Glasgow, Newcastle, Stourbridge, Whittington, and Waterford. The most important centres were London, Waterford, Bristol and Birmingham. Later there were glass-cutting works at York, Leith and Portobello. About eighty years ago there were glass-works at Hull.

Mr. Hartshorne in his book on "Old English Glasses" divides drinking glasses, roughly speaking, into two great groups: tavern glass, coarse; and do-

*Littel's Living Age: "Gentlemen Glassmakers."*

mestic glass, fine. These two groups are again sub-divided according to the shapes of the bowls. Mr. Bate, on the other hand, bases his classification on the stems, beginning with baluster which was the first to make its appearance. In Figure 58 is shown a group of baluster stems covering a period of two centuries, the seventeenth and eighteenth. There are drawn, blown, moulded and one cut stem; the domed folded foot, and a variety of knops and balusters which were used. These glasses belong to the Victoria and Albert Museum, London.

After the baluster came successively, drawn, air twist, white twist and cut stems. All these styles of stems overlapped, just as in old furniture there was no absolutely definite time for an abrupt change in style. One faded into another. It is true that as early as 1760 cut stems appeared on glasses, but plain stems also persisted and so did twisted stems.

In addition to the stems as a means of dating specimens, the way the foot was made also gave indication of the period of manufacture. The earliest foot had the edge turned back or folded over on itself all around— you can see this in Figure 58—the width of the fold varying from one-quarter to one-half inch. The Venetian method of folding the foot was the reverse of the English, for they folded it downward and underneath.

The pontil mark left rough is another indication of age. In fact the rough pontil mark existed on glasses

*Figure 58, page 115.*

till the stage of cut stems, then the roughness was smoothed off, leaving a circular depressed mark on the bottom of the vessel.

The classification of wine glasses according to the shape of the bowl, made by Mr. Hartshorne and enlarged by Mr. Bate, is given below, but American collectors need to have a coloured stem, or some peculiarity of cut or ornamentation, to induce them to add wine glasses to their collections. The shapes of the bowls are classed as: drawn, bell, waisted bell, straight sided, straight sided rectangular, ovoid, ogee, lipped ogee, double ogee and waisted.

The classification of stems seems so much easier for the collector who may wish to add a few examples of English drinking glasses to his collection, that I give it here. Excluding the baluster stems which have already been given, there are: first, drawn; second, air twist; third, cotton twist; fourth, cut. Examples of these four groups are given in Figure 59.

The air twist or tear, as it is called, is the pear-shaped air bubble which is found within the stem. These tears may be long and attenuated, fat and squatty, with the point turning up or down, according to the fancy of the maker.

If the glass has what is known as the drawn stem, the method of manufacture was to draw the metal for the stem out from the bowl. When the stem was decorated with an air twist, the stems were sometimes made

*Figure 59, page 116.*

of glass rods which could be easily cut up into small pieces and to which the bowl of the glass and the foot were welded.

These small bubbles of air called tears became under the manipulation of a skillful workman a decoration of great beauty. The air twist stems were in vogue for a long time, till 1780 at least. The decoration of the stems was so in demand that about the middle of the eighteenth century the glass men looked about for new methods. The opaque or cotton stems exist on dated specimens from as early as 1745. These twisted opaque stems were made by welding together slender canes of opaque glass, placing them in the centre of a mould and then pouring molten glass about them. The stem was then revolved and drawn out according to the fancy of the workmen, and there resulted twisted stems of endless variety. Towards the end of the century, say about 1780, coloured glass rods were introduced. General Washington, who was always on the lookout for the "newest fashion" in table appointments, evidently fancied the coloured twist. There is a small wine glass at Mount Vernon which belonged to him, with scarlet and white threads in the stem. Also one at the Smithsonian Museum at Washington, where are numerous specimens of the elegancies in which General Washington indulged.

An interesting fact stated by Mr. Bate concerning these wine glasses with twisted stems either white or coloured, is that the pontil mark is never smoothed off in authentic specimens. In many more or less recent forgeries it is smoothly cut away. There were many of these glasses with twisted coloured stems made at Bristol, England. Blue, that entrancing shade of sapphire blue which we associate with Bristol, was of course largely used. Yellow and white were frequently used too, and a pale shade of lavender, rarely.

Late in the eighteenth century cutting began to appear on the stems, and wine glasses in two shades of green, with or without cut flutes, began to be popular. Then came the glasses with coloured bowls mounted on clear stems, a charming style, which is just coming in again, and being put on the market in very beautiful metal by some of our own glass-works. Mr. Bate in his book, "English Table Glass," gives 1758 as the earliest dated wine glass with a cut stem which he has ever come across, and he believes that most of the cut stem wine glasses date between 1775 and 1800.

The glass of this period, clear, hard and lustrous, presented a surface capable of taking on the finest decoration. The use of the wheel enabled the cutters and polishers to bring their art to the highest perfection. They no longer allowed the blemish of the rough pontil mark to deface their choice productions, so this mark is often cut away, leaving a smooth circular spot.

The English collector is able to acquire other glasses of more or less interest and beauty which seldom come into the hands of the American collector: tall slender ale glasses, the stems following the general designs of those found in wine glasses of the same period. There were many kinds of ale. Cock, stepony, sage-ale, stitch-back, college ale, china ale and butler's ale. The decoration of these ale glasses was very pretty, a wreath of hops or barley, or sometimes just a single spray done in the best style of the cutter's art.

The goblet crowded out the ale glass of which it is a close connection, the chief difference between the two being the greater width and consequently greater capacity of the goblet. The makers of these vessels seem to have gone to the extreme and produced goblets which were capable of holding one, two or even three quarts of liquor. It might be remarked in passing that the stems of these gigantic glasses were heavily knopped or cut to render them less liable to slip through uncertain fingers.

That a great variety of wines contributed to this uncertainty can be proved by the fact that during the XVI, XVII and XVIII centuries the following wines could be obtained in England in addition to other strong drinks not here set down. There were "claret, red wyne, whit wyne, Frenche wyne, New Gascon, wyne of Graves, Olde Frenche, Muscadyne, Rynishe, Maumsey, Bastard, Cherys, Wyne of Galeake, Romanye, Aligant, Canary, Malligo, Epicrist, Sweet Spanish, Rochelle, Bordeaux, Bayonne, Deale, Piment, Hippocras, Port, Portgual wine and Caliavela."

Sir John English in "Country Lasses," 1715, writes:

"Will your grace taste a glass of old hock, with a little, little dash of palm, before you eat? A Seville orange squeezed into a glass of noble, racy old canary? Or a glass of your right Southam cyder, sweetened with a little old mead and a hard toast?"

The forerunner of the cocktail, no doubt.

Many of these wines were rendered more palate tickling by the addition of spices. They might be touched up with cinnamon, mace or cloves; they might have a scraping of nutmeg, galingal or coriander; and there were also caraways, aniseed, ginger and pepper, together with honey.

Besides the wine and ale glasses and the huge goblets there were small glasses similar in shape to the goblets, called dram glasses. Rummers, much in shape like the goblets, were not only used for rum, but for grog, toddy, punch and all the other drinks, including home-brewed cider. Some distinctive cider glasses have as decoration an apple blossom, or a bunch of the fruit, or a border of fruit and leaves.

Occasionally charming glass mugs are to be found, more often in coloured glass than in clear. But the decoration is far superior on the clear glass mugs to that on the coloured glass, since it is engraving of hop vines, leaves, sometimes birds and occasionally the name of the owner. I have a particular fancy for glass mugs coloured or clear, preferably the former. It is a fact that these charming objects, often quite small, are, in the case of the coloured specimens, frequently defaced by crude ornamentation in enamel. I have tried to remove this enamel from specimens by every known means in my power, but it cannot be done without defacing the mug. But the white glass mugs do not have the decorative value of the coloured ones, so I turn my mugs about so as to see as little of the so-called decoration as possible.

In many of these glasses the convivial habits of the topers was given thought to. The desire to pound on the table which would annihilate any delicate glass, could be indulged in with impunity with those solid and heavy stemmed drinking glasses. Some of those furnished at coaching houses had no stem at all, the customer being expected to drain it before setting it down.

Very beautiful candlesticks of clear glass following in shape the cut and knopped stems of the wine glasses and with heavy cut or domed foot, are sometimes met with. Other objects in clear glass are pitchers, salt cellars, covered cups, sugar basins, bowls and sweetmeat glasses; these are sometimes found and are always interesting. There were other things too, paperweights, scent bottles, inkstands and even canes and pipes.

In one of Cumberland's plays, "The Natural Son,"

written about 1765, one of the characters says: "I re-member I broke a glass hoop ring, which it was then the fashion to wear, into your finger, by squeezing your hand."

A type of glass which must have been used for sweet-meats, custard or some other food which could have been eaten out of it with a spoon, is often charming in shape and decoration. Mr. Hartshorne calls them champagne glasses, which seems a curious error, since it is impossible to drink out of them without spilling the contents, on account of the flaring rim. Besides being flaring this rim is often indented or deeply cut, a still further impediment to comfortable imbibing. But for whatever purpose they were intended they are very ornamental, and well worth a place in any cabinet.

Gin glasses with very small bowls of very thick glass are sought by collectors. They were made between 1736-43, when the tax on this liquor was very high, so that even a small amount was costly. After 1743, though some of the heavy duties were removed the price continued to rise, so that it still remained costly. In 1751 gin, though still taxed, was not hard to get. In a magazine of that day called "The Connoisseur," a writer says: "Madam Gin has been christened by as many names as a German princess. Every petty chan-dler's shop will sell you 'Sky Blue,' and every night cellar will furnish you with 'Holland Tape.' Nor can I see the difference between 'Oil of Venus,' 'Spirit of

Fig. 62. ADAM CHANDELIERS

(*See page* 150)

Fig. 63.  STANDING LIGHTS
Fig. 64.  BRISTOL GLASS

(*See pages* 151 *and* 155)

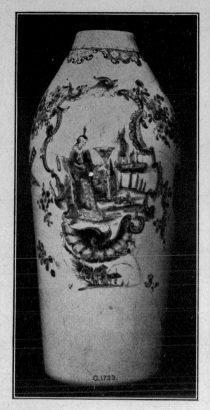

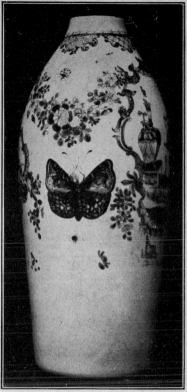

Fig. 65.  BRISTOL VASE        Fig. 66.  BRISTOL VASE, REVERSE

(*See page* 155)

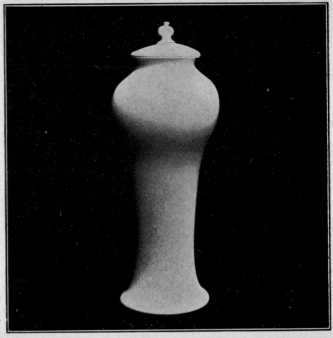

Fig. 67. BRISTOL COVERED JAR
Fig. 68. BRISTOL CUT GLASS BOWI

*(See page* 156)

Fig. 69. BRISTOL BLUE GLASS

(See page 156)

Fig. 70.  PAPER-WEIGHT

Fig. 71.  NAILSEA FLASKS

(*See pages* 158 *and* 170)

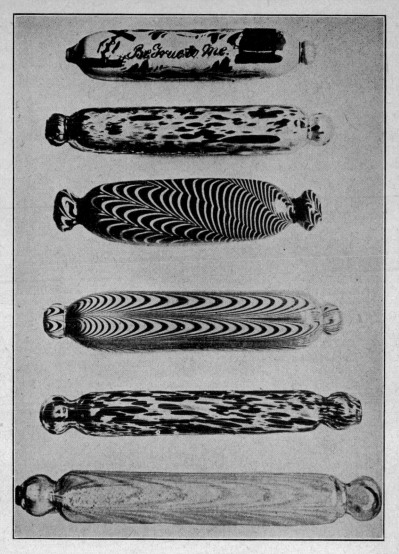

Fig. 72. ROLLING-PINS

(See page 170)

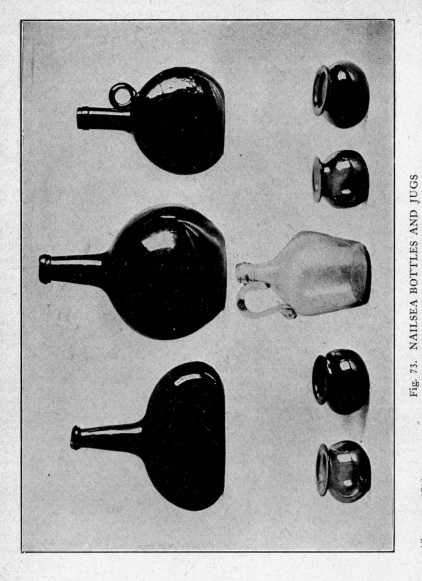

Fig. 73. NAILSEA BOTTLES AND JUGS

(*See page 171*)

Adona,' and 'Parfait Amour,' for the use of our quality, and what among the vulgar is called 'Cupid's Eye-water,' 'Strip me Naked,' and 'Lay me Down Softly.' "

Besides these drinking glasses of all descriptions there were many vastly more beautiful objects made, generally in rich cut glass and often mounted in silver or Sheffield plate. Tea caddies of glass heavily cut were mounted in silver with silver handles and lock. Punch bowls with the edges cut in squares so that the glasses could be hung on were made of silver or plate; Sheffield and Birmingham made many of them. They were often called monteiths, though the original monteiths were made to wash glasses, not to hold liquor, and were named after the inventor.

"New things produce new words, and thus Monteth
Has by one vessel saved his name from death."

Coloured glass bottles are sometimes found of the size and shape of Worcestershire sauce bottles, and with Sheffield plate screw tops. I found one recently, and the plate was worn down to the copper in spots. Epergnes, table ornaments of many kinds, girandoles and table lights, were often combined with plate. Although they were made in several places in England, both glass and mountings, it is customary for those who own them to call the glass Waterford, and the plate Sheffield!

In Sir James Yoxall's little book, "Collecting Old

Glass," he gives seven tests which the collector should apply to the piece before he buys it.

> One. The tint of the glass.
> Two. The sound of the glass.
> Three. The quality of the glass metal.
> Four. The weight.
> Five. Signs of use and wear.
> Six. Pontil Mark.
> Seven. Workmanship.

To my mind there is nothing so necessary for the would-be collector as experience, and by this I mean the handling of much glass of which the history is known. After you learn the peculiar tint of old glass of English and Irish make particularly, the weight of the object seems to me to be of great importance.

A book on "English Baluster Stemmed Glasses of the Seventeenth and Eighteenth Centuries," by Francis Buckley, has this to say about the weight of those glasses: "English made glasses of the first period were all light in weight and cloudy in appearance. Some time between the Restoration and the end of the seventeenth century, but when precisely it is difficult to say, the English glass-makers began to try experiments with a view to removing from their glass this dull and cloudy appearance. Their object was to produce a substance like crystal; and this object they eventually achieved by introducing into their metal a large quantity of lead. This gave the characteristic weight."

Of course when you come to consider weight, you

must take into consideration the class of the object, blown glass being light while cut glass cut from the block, and much moulded glass is heavy. If the moulded glass is blown into a mould, not pressed in mechanically, it may be as light in weight as blown glass. Old moulded glass is often extremely beautiful, more attractive when in coloured glass, than when it is cut.

There are collectors who claim to be able to tell the difference between English and Irish glass by the patterns used in the cutting. But this test does not always prove satisfactory, for the glass-cutters copied from each other patterns which became popular. Both English and Irish cutters used hobnail, diamond, strawberry and pomegranate cutting. The Stourbridge cutting was as a rule deep, regular, less free and flowing than the work on Irish glass, and less attractive than the Bristol cutting, which was deep, to be sure, but in free designs as well. The thistle cutting of Newcastle consisted of small diamond-shaped design upon glasses which somewhat resembled the thistle in form.

The pomegranate, a favourite, was often combined with diamond cutting. The star on the bottom of old glass is usually on the bottom of the base, extending to the edge. In modern glass the star is generally smaller.

In that most comprehensive book by Dudley Westropp, "Irish Glass," to which all students of this subject are deeply indebted, he has this to say with reference to English glass-workers in Ireland:

"It must be remembered that most of the glass-works set up in Ireland were erected by Englishmen, who would naturally introduce English forms and cutting, and who would also use the same materials that they had been accustomed to employ in England. In the report of the committee appointed in 1785 to enquire into the commercial relations between Great Britain and Ireland, John Holmes, flint-glass manufacturer, Whitefriars, London, stated that three-quarters of the glass workmen in Ireland were emigrants from England, and that the masters of four of the Irish glass-houses were Englishmen."

He also states that when the Waterford and Cork glass-houses were established, all the workmen and materials were brought over from England. Workmen were constantly going back and forth to Ireland, and the report goes on to say that "Mr. Hill, a great manufacturer at Stourbridge, had lately gone to Waterford, and taken the best set of workmen he could get in the County of Worcester." The number of men that Mr. Hill took is later stated to be "eight or ten," and the report also states that numbers of skilled workmen went to Ireland and France.

Yet there are people who declare that they can distinguish English glass from Irish!

As for the glass made in other Irish centres besides

Waterford, Mr. Westropp says: "The glass-house set up at Drumrea, near Dungannon, and also the one at Belfast, were both carried on by Benjamin Edwards, a Bristol glass-maker, and as we have seen, the Cork and Waterford factories were worked by Stourbridge glass-makers, and obtained all their materials from England. Thus the glass made, during the early period at least, at Cork and Waterford, would be simply Stourbridge glass made in these towns, and that made at Drumrea and Belfast would be very similar to Bristol glass. The Drumrea glass-house used local sand, which may have caused a slight difference in the metal, but for the Belfast glass-works the sand used during the eighteenth century would probably have been obtained from the same source as that for the Bristol works."

But though the question of where this lovely old glass was made is most intricate, the collector has a great range of objects to choose from, most of them far more pleasing than the wine glasses which appeal so strongly to the English collector, and which need a whole chronological series to be of any great interest.

Great quantities of English glass were sent to America. As early as August, 1719, there was a "Glass Shop" in Queen Street, Boston, which advertised in the *Boston News Letter* of that date. By fifty years later the objects in glass to be bought at all the large centres in this country were immense in number. Leaving out most of the different wine glasses, there were to be found: "cream jugs, syllabub and sweetmeat glasses, cruet stands, flowered wine and water glasses, glass salvers, small enamelled shank wine glasses, flowered, scalloped and plain decanters, jugs and mugs, salver and pyramids, glasses for silver, salts and sweetmeats, poles with spires and glasses, smelling bottles, sconces, tulip and flower glasses of the newest patterns, finger basins and tumblers of all sorts."

There were also made at the various English factories and on sale here, punch, salad and trifle bowls, punch lifters, custard glasses and stands, flip glasses, fruit baskets, epergnes, tazzas, sugar bowls with or without covers, castors, nightlight glasses, wine coolers, pickle and mustard jars, preserve pots, vases, standing cups and covers, butter pots, celery glasses, weather glasses, witch balls, holy water vessels, posset pots, door-stops, paper-weights, lustres, spill holders, toy birds and animals, glass eggs and gazing balls.

Sets of glass ware as well as sets of china were held in great esteem, and such a set with diamond cutting is shown in Figure 60. Salt-cellars form a most attractive subject for the collector, beginning with those with oval bowls, standing on short stems and heavily cut. These come not only in clear glass, but in blue and ruby as well but very rarely in green. Bristol turned out some most attractive striped ones, and Ireland very heavy ones richly cut. The collector who

*Figure 60, page 117.*

has the opportunity to frequent antique shops and auction sales, and a long deep purse, has a chance to follow almost any hobby in the glass line.

Millefiori paper-weights, whether of Venetian, Bristol, French or New Jersey make, are most attractive, but we do bar those made in Kansas! These paper-weights have risen hugely in cost during the last year or two. The paper-weights vary exceedingly in size, colouring, details of manufacture and beauty, but they are almost all interesting, and offer a wide field for what is, after all, one of the chief delights of collecting, speculation as to where the piece was made, when, who owned it, and those thousand and one reflections which float through your mind as you finger these silent records of other days. It might be stated right here that not only were paper-weights made in this millefiori ware, but inkstands and pepper-pots as well. I have seen both these objects and they are always of very superior workmanship: that is, the mosaic arrangement is composed of very small pieces and the colouring rich. The pepper-pots have pewter tops which do not screw on but have a hinge and snap.

In Figure 61 is a mantle set for candles with cut glass prisms. These were very popular and no woman considered the best room or parlour complete without a set of lustres, as they were called, in which she burned wax candles when company came, bayberry dips not being considered choice enough.

*Figure 61, page 118.*

There were also chandeliers and wall-lights in plain crystal or crystal and coloured glass, many of them made during the Adam period and based on their designs, therefore of simple and elegant patterns. Some are shown in Figure 62. It is claimed that Waterford alone made pear-shaped drops for chandeliers and wall-lights, but many chandeliers which I have examined, and which are known to have been of English make, were also decorated with the same shaped drops.

The large crystal chandelier which has been suspended from the ceiling in the Declaration Room of Independence Hall, Philadelphia, for upward of two centuries, and which was recently removed, has been cleaned and restrung and its beauty is attracting much attention from visitors.

When the plans were drawn up by the Philadelphia Chapter of the American Institute of Architects providing for restoration of Independence Hall to its original condition it was determined to retain the chandelier on account of its historical value. The records in the possession of Wilfred Jordan, curator of Independence Hall, show that the candle fixture was placed in the room in which the Declaration of Independence was signed to illuminate the chamber at the night session held by the Continental Congress.

The chandelier was made at Waterford, Ireland, and imported to America in 1760. It is considered by ex-

*Figure 62, page 135.*

perts to-day to be one of the finest chandeliers of its kind in the world.

The standing lights shown in Figure 63 are most decorative. These were made for candles and were extremely brilliant when lighted. In fact the beauty of glass for use in lighting effects has been known for centuries, and though occasionally a fad for some other medium comes up it does not last long. The study of prisms alone provokes surprise, for the variety of them is immense. They may be in one, two, or three sections, the commonest form being two. They may be either cut or pressed, be square on the bottom or pointed, and no matter what form they take are always ornamental. Occasionally they are cut on the back in diamond or small point design. I have a turquoise glass spill holder with prisms hanging from the fluted rim. These are in two sections and are very prettily cut in small points on the back, and have long slender points on the ends.

Occasionally the prism may be clear glass with coloured points. I have seen them with both green and blue points, in the latter case they were on a lamp of clear glass heavily engraved. There are also to be found prisms, so called, cut from thick coloured glass in a conventional leaf shape. They are called "English" but are a device of the faker to charm the unwary.

*Figure 63, page 136.*

THE history of Bristol, known as a "trade town," began about the year 1000, when a small Saxon settlement grew up at the junction of the rivers Frome and Avon. Wool, which was exported to the Baltic, a wine trade with France, soap-making and tanning were the earliest industries. Later, from about 1377 to 1488, the wool trade was supplanted by the cloth trade, the rich and powerful Society of Merchant Venturers was established, and the voyages of John and Sebastian Cabot took place. In the sixteenth century Bristol traded with Spain, the Canaries, the Spanish colonies in America, and began traffic in slaves.

By the eighteenth century the chief aids to the prosperity of the city were the manufactures of iron, brass, tin and copper and the flourishing slave trade, West Indian sugar being taken in exchange for African slaves.*

The glass and china trade never grew of sufficient importance to be reckoned as one of the great industries of Bristol, though shipments of both these goods were sent to the different countries where there were trade relations.

In May, 1696, there were ninety glass-houses in

* "Little Red Book of Bristol," etc.

England, twenty-four of these being in London, nine at Bristol, seventeen at Stourbridge, and eleven at Newcastle.*

Queen Anne visited Bristol in 1702 and the Corporation of the City gave her a dinner; among the expense items enumerated was six pounds and fourteen shillings for glass.

The troubles of the Bristol glass-makers began early. In Latimer's "Annals of Bristol," he writes: "a fiscal interference with the glass trade, exciting much local irritation, was resolved upon by the Government during the session (1728). With the object of preventing smuggling, the importation of wine in bottles and small casks was absolutely prohibited. The Bristol glass-makers petitioned against the proposal, asserting that many thousand persons were employed in making bottles for exportation, which were re-imported filled with wine, and that the stoppage of the business would cause entire destruction of the bottle trade; but the protest was ineffectual."

When the Duke of York visited the Bristol glass-houses on December 27, 1761, the black bottle, flint and plate glass manufacturers occupied fifteen large glass-houses, some of them being entirely confined to bottle-making.†

On August 22, 1789, Wadham, Ricketts and Company opened the Phoenix Flint Glass Works, which

* Houghton's Letters.
† Evans: "History of Bristol."

works still exist under the firm name of Powell and Ricketts. The story of Bristol glass-making, like that of most other glass-making centres, is mixed up with that of other towns where glass was made. Men from Birmingham came to both Bristol and Nailsea—they were only nine miles apart—and some of the Bristol men went to Sunderland, where the firm of Hartleys was established in 1836.

It might be well to state here that some of the most effective forgeries of Bristol and Nailsea glass are made at or near Birmingham, very skillfully aged by the use of acids. Birmingham has long been in the business of making coloured glass, for in December, 1830, Jonathan Wright of Waterford, Ireland, wrote that he was not only going to have the finest shop in Waterford "but was getting in some coloured glass and other things from Birmingham." *

Bristol made fine table glass, transparent, and besides the crystal, made it in blue, greenish blue, purple, and red. It is well to remember that Bristol red glass is of the ruby hue, with less vermilion in it than the Bohemian product. They also made what they called "cherry-red" glass.†

Much of the Bristol glass had lines, sprigs and floral designs on it in gold, and these wore off if the object was much handled. I have a water bottle, double ogee in shape, in dark blue glass which has little sprigs

* Westropp: "Irish Glass."
† Yoxall: "Collecting Old Glass."

in gold scattered all over it. These sprigs are all worn off around the neck, and on that part of the body where the hand rested in lifting the bottle.

Sir James Yoxall in his little book, "Collecting Old Glass," says that nobody can be sure from which place, Bristol or Nailsea, came any particular bauble. They both made flasks, witch balls, rolling-pins, mugs and jugs, pipes and canes, scent bottles, hats and other trifles. In Figure 64 the two dark pieces waved and flecked with white are in the Bristol Museum, England, and marked "Bristol." The theory is that the brighter pieces are Bristol, the more delicate and refined glass, Nailsea, like the third bottle of clear glass with white lines.

There are collectors who particularly esteem the opaque white glass which imitates as closely as possible, at least in decoration, Oriental china. The most desirable pieces were decorated by Michael Edkins, formerly a painter of Delftware. Painting on china proved not so profitable as painting on glass, apparently, and between the years 1762 and 1787, no fewer than five glass firms of repute engaged him.

Some of his work, done at the glass-works of Little and Longman, Redcliff Back, is shown in Figures 65 and 66. It reveals how closely the Chinese style was copied. The English decorator was very partial to the tall Oriental figures which he called "long Elizas" and which were very decorative. Whistler once

*Figures 64, 65 and 66, pages 136 and 137.*

painted a picture which he named "Langen Lizen," and which at one time was owned in this country.

The opaque covered jar in Figure 67 is a lovely thing, all the better perhaps without decoration. These opaque pieces and the very heavily cut glass bowl in Figure 68, Bristol also, are in the Bristol Museum, England. This cut glass bowl, or basin as the English prefer to call it, is for sugar, and is only four and a half inches high.

Collectors in America are as a rule more eager for the clear, vivid royal blue glass made at Bristol. These pieces are sometimes decorated with spiral lines of white glass which ends in a white rim, and sometimes with a white rim alone like pieces occasionally met with in this country. They made odd pieces of this blue glass, such as twisted snakes flecked with gold, and little hats all in the plain blue. Many of these rich blue pieces were decorated as well as made by Isaac Jacobs, whose father Lazarus had a glass-house in Temple Street, Bristol, from 1785 to 1787. Isaac was glass manufacturer to His Majesty George III, and seems to have continued in business till 1821. Pieces of royal blue glass signed by him are in the Bristol Museum.

The peculiar richness of this Bristol blue glass is said to be due to the presence of antimony, which gives depth of color and great brilliancy. In Figure 69 are shown some pieces of this blue Bristol glass which are in the

*Figures 67, 68 and 69, pages 138 and 139.*

Pennsylvania Museum. The covered bowl in a stand is unusually fine. The bowl has the white edge spoken of before, and is engraved on the side, "Bristol, 1812."

The little mug beside it is an attractive example of these small objects. I have one like it, exquisite in color, but thickly strewn with tiny air bubbles which were the result of insufficient "cooking" of the metal. A crude little wreath of flowers is on the front of my mug, a very common form of decoration. Sometimes they just daubed little streaks of red, blue and yellow and let it go at that. This decoration on my piece is not enamel but in some kind of mineral paint which wears off somewhat with use.

Bristol in its palmy days boasted no less than fifteen glass-houses, and had no rival as to quality or output. This was in 1760. About a hundred years earlier an order by the City Council was to the effect that "no stranger or foreigner should presume to open a shop, either with or without glass windows, under a penalty of five pounds."

Bristol made imitation of Venetian glass to such perfection that Sidney J. Lewis in his book, "Old Glass and How to Collect It," says: "Many a collection hailing ostensibly from Venice, must on close scrutiny be attributed to a place of origin much nearer home. This form of substitution was particularly prevalent in the case of glass ornamented with white twisted threads, and in the case of ruby-coloured glasses and mugs."

There were made at Bristol cups, mugs, salt-cellars, small bowls, finger basins, vases both open and covered, candlesticks and taper sticks, flasks, bells, canes, paper-weights, etc. I own a paper-weight, Figure 70, which I believe was made at Bristol. It is of unusual type. On an oblong base reclines a typical British bull-dog and the whole piece is in that rarely beautiful shade of deep blue. The piece is very heavy, and the dog was made in a mould and added to the base, the undercutting showing plainly. There are signs of much wear on the base and two or three chips, but the dog is perfect.

Many glass paper-weights were made at Bristol sixty or seventy years ago, which are not at all easy to find now, although it is said that they have been made again in recent years. They show a cameo of glass, silvered, mounted upon a lump of clear glass, and the effect is quite pleasing. Sometimes these glass cameos were placed on vases, generally of highly coloured opaque glass. Occasionally they are brought down from top shelves of store closets where they have defied time and the rummage sale for several generations.

These silvered cameos were invented by Apsley Pellat (born 1791, died 1863) and he called them "crystallo ceramie." It was a species of glass incrustation, and they were not only applied to paper-weights and vases, but to bottles, decanters, snuff-boxes, lustres for lights and rings. The cameos were made of a compo-

*Figure 70, page 140.*

Fig. 74.  CANDELABRA

(*See page* 179)

Fig. 75. DECANTER, MARKED "PENROSE"

(*See page* 182)

Fig. 76. JUGS, PROBABLY WATERFORD

(See page 191)

Fig. 77. BOWL AND CELERY GLASS

Fig. 78.  WATERFORD GLASS

Fig. 79.  WATERFORD AND CORK TUMBLERS

(*See page* 192)

Fig. 80. GOBLETS, WATERFORD

(See page 192)

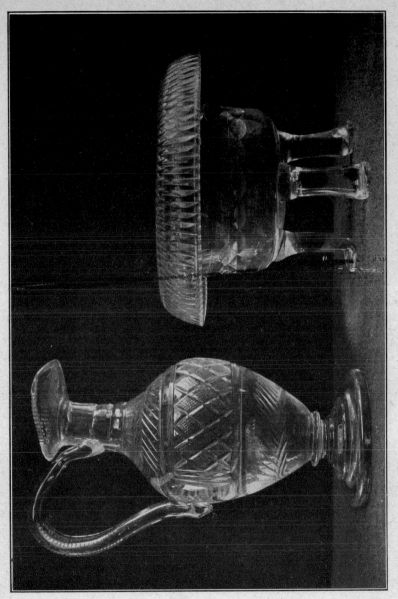

Fig. 81. DUBLIN OR CORK GLASS

*(See page 196)*

Fig. 82. BOAT-SHAPE AND TURNOVER BOWLS

(See page 197)

sition of china clay and super-silicate of potash, which was able to stand a higher degree of heat than the glass upon which they were superimposed. It is odd how few of them have survived.

Bottles for water and decanters of this same entrancing shade of blue spoken of before are not hard to find. I have a couple, one with a chain of gilt painted about its neck, and an oval mark enclosing the word "shrub." There is a pretty stopper, oval in shape and having a few lines of gilt on it. The second bottle is of the same shape but greater capacity and of a finer quality glass, perfectly cooked so that there are no air bubbles; both of them have collared necks.

Of course to show this coloured glass to best advantage it must be displayed against the light. Arranged in a window on glass shelves, against ground glass, so that there is a clear opaque background for it, it is very ornamental.

Door-stops were also made at Bristol as well as at other places. The Bristol ones were of a clear shade of green with many air bubbles in them, which looked something like a fountain. Some of these door-stops in addition to being flattened on the bottom were also flat on one side so as to rest against the door. Paper-weights of this same shade of green glass were also a Bristol product. They often had in them lily-like flowers and some of them were five or six inches tall.

The dolphin as an ornament on glass probably originated in Venice. A single dolphin in exquisite opal glass, bearing on his tail a shallow flaring dish, shell-like in shape, is not a rare Italian model. Twisted dolphins were used in England as well as single ones, and sometimes they were used on covers. Later the dolphin was much used in the various Sandwich patterns of pressed glass.

The little bird as a cover ornament is also Italian, English, and then American, showing how the glass-makers copied anything they thought attractive no matter where they found it. These little birds on top of a covered mug are very graceful, even if the shape of the bird is somewhat crude.

The influence of the Bristol glass-makers was more far-reaching than is commonly suspected. Mr. Westropp gives credit to Bristol glass-makers for establishing glass-works in Ireland, and Mr. Hunter in his book, "Stiegel Glass," speaks of Stiegel following the "Bristol tradition." There are articles known to have been made by Stiegel, for example some of the covered bowls and other objects in transparent blue glass with a rim of white glass which are precisely like those made at Bristol.

## NAILSEA GLASS

THE town of Nailsea where glass-making flourished for eighty-five years, finally closing its doors in 1873, is in Somerset, and in the Bristol district. This accounts for its productions being so often classed as old Bristol glass, and for the fact that there is so little on record having reference to Nailsea alone.

The works, called the "Nailsea Glass Works," were opened in 1788 by John Robert Lucas, who was a son of Robert Lucas, a glass bottle manufacturer of Bristol, who died 1775.

In 1793 the firm of Lucas, Chance, Homer and Coathupe was established at Nailsea, and the business must have been profitable, for in 1807 when the partnership was renewed the firm had a capital of sixty thousand pounds, and in addition to the crown glass works at Nailsea, owned at least two other works at other places, and had an office and warehouse at Bristol.

In 1810 Robert Lucas Chance became manager of the works, and from that time on the firm passed through different hands, till in 1836 it became the well-known firm of Chance Bros. and Co.* There were after this many more changes in ownership, till, curi-

* *The Connoisseur,* 1911: "Nailsea Glass."

ously enough, the firm name became again in 1870 Chance Bros. and Co., and they carried on the business till 1873, when the works were closed. There have been many reasons given for the closing of the works in 1873, but as only sheet and rolled plate glass were made there then, the reason probably was that they did not pay.

The Nailsea glass which is of interest to collectors shows specimens very beautiful in color, like the ornamental flasks which were Nailsea's chief product; a few of them are shown in Figure 71. The flask with the top in this figure is Venetian, and shows where the inspiration for the Nailsea flasks came from. Objects more or less quaint, like the rolling-pins, Figure 72, were made in numbers, and there were jugs, pipes, bells and some pieces known as "freaks," which it is supposed the workmen made and sold on their own account.

The flasks display the well-known ribbon or latticinio effects, made popular by the French and Venetian workmen who moved from one factory to another. These charming flasks vary in height from three and a quarter to about ten and a half inches. A few of them have the double neck which was so characteristic of Venice. Nearly every colour was employed, clear and opaque, white, brown, yellow, red, pink, salmon, and greens and blue, both dark and light. The rolling-pins had knops at the ends, and generally one of these could be opened to put in flour or water to

*Figures 71 and 72, pages 140 and 141.*

give it weight. Many of them are beautifully ribboned while there are also plain coloured ones of dark glass with such pious mottoes as, "May the eye of the Lord watch ever," presumably to keep the user from skimping on the recipe, or from using "just as goods."

There were bottles and jugs spotted and striped, the decoration crude, but the shapes of the bottles very attractive. Every collector of old glass, no matter how dainty and fanciful the objects he gathers, smuggles in somewhere one or two of those delightful wide-bodied bottles, often in a rich dark green glass, or in brown or a pale bluish green, clear glass. Nailsea made these Falstaffian-bodied objects in these colours; see Figure 73. A few have been found in the dark green with white striping.

Glass bells were some of the choicest of their products. They were very decorative if not very useful. Some were of ruby tint with clear glass clappers, and handles of greenish-white opaque glass with a knob on top of peacock blue.

The old-time potworks in various parts of England were worked by a rough crew which came from all parts of Europe. In the days of the great Wedgwood, Burslem, Etruria, in fact all the "Five Towns" as the great pottery centres were called, were subjects of great concern as to their morals and manners, both of which were bad. The great preacher Whitfield went down

*Figure 73, page 142.*

to conduct meetings, and, to say the least, was not favourably received.

The glass-works at Nailsea were as bad. It is recorded that in 1792 the glass-house people lived in nineteen cottages, nearly two hundred of them, and that they were herded in together, both sexes and all ages. They called themselves "savages" or "heads," and to such as came to minister to them were as rough as the potters. They called their group of hovels "Little Hell" or "Botany Bay." It is stated that Hannah and Martha Moore, religious teachers, had considerable success taming these savages, but that is as it may be.

Such people were of course superstitious, so they made hollow glass balls, sometimes as large as seven inches in diameter, which were intended as charms to ward off the Evil Eye. They were gaudy things daubed on the inside with many colours. Yet I have seen one of these Nailsea balls hanging in a window (which was where the Nailsea men put them) on the Massachusetts coast, looking out to sea, which was a thing of beauty. It is a very rich blue, flecked with white, and has the pleasing effect which all these Nailsea objects have. The makers may have been rough, tough personages, but the work of their hands was admirable.

The style of glass produced at Nailsea was undoubtedly Venetian with its latticinio effects. The native workmen were taught by French and Venetian glass-blowers who went from one factory to another.

Many of the Frenchmen lived at Nailsea, and a row of cottages was built for them known as "French Rank." Glass-workers are very liable to chest diseases and snails were considered a panacea. The Bristol glass-workers probably contracted the taste for them from the Nailsea Frenchmen, for they still eat them.*

Another thing which the Nailsea glass men made for health's sake, was a long glass tube or cane, sometimes a yard to eight feet long, which they set up in their houses and wiped clean every morning, so that the diseases which gathered on it could be wiped away. If the rod was broken, that house which owned it was marked for misfortune.

So attractive is this old Nailsea glass that there are many forged pieces of it on the market. Jugs, bottles, bowls of a poor quality glass with wide, wavy, white lines are to be found in abundance with positive assurance from the sellers that they are "old Nailsea." It is well to remember that the objects made at Nailsea were almost always small, and that they are rarely to be met with in this country. None of the pieces shown in the illustrations are above ten inches tall.

* *The Connoisseur:* "Nailsea Glass."

THE story of Irish glass is an interesting one, and romantic as well. So little has been known about the Irish factories and their product that bit by bit legends have grown up about them, particularly Waterford. It is curious how quickly the facts about an industry seem to vanish, even one which was as prosperous in its day as Waterford in Ireland, or Sandwich, in America.

But while all old Irish glass is interesting and in most cases beautiful, more interest seems to attach to what was made in Waterford than to that made at either Cork, Dublin or Belfast. But this is really only a fanciful notion, for in Ireland as in all glass-making centres, the workmen travelled about from one place to another, using the same materials for the metal, the same patterns for the objects they made, and the same designs for decoration. The Cork Glass Cutter's Union had a fine device on their membership cards, and the motto upon it was, "A Pleasant Road and a Cheerful Welcome to Every Tramp."

It is only within the last few years that the true history of Irish glass has been patiently dug out of old records, newspapers, account books and family histories. This task has been performed by M. S. Dudley

Westropp, lately of the National Museum of Ireland, who has done for Irish glass what Mr. Hartshorne did for English glass.

For the collector it is unfortunate that this Irish glass has been so eagerly sought. It has paid the forger to reproduce it, and to get hold of plain pieces which are real antiques and cut them in the old patterns, so that the result is not unlike the spurious French statues of the Gothic period which have deceived Museum experts both in Europe and America.

You will constantly hear it stated that it is possible to distinguish real old Waterford glass by its blue tint, owing to the presence of lead. This is not so. Mr. Westropp in his book, "Irish Glass," says: "With the exception of a few drawings of some of the patterns used in the Waterford glass-house, no others belonging to Irish glass-works are known to exist." He next says that "Waterford glass has not the blue tint hitherto ascribed to it. This in itself stamps as spurious hundreds of pieces which have been accepted as genuine Waterford. . . . If all the alleged Waterford glass in existence were genuine, despite the output of the factory and allowing for the amount that has been broken, it would have taken probably two or three glass-houses to produce it."

Something like the amount of stuff that descendants claim came over in the *Mayflower!*

But it is true that there are varying tints in this old

glass. When placed upon a white cloth, much of the old cut-glass has what might be called a darkling tint, not exactly bluish, nor blackish either, but something entirely different from the colour of modern cut-glass, no matter what its origin.

There is in the Smithsonian Museum in Washington a very handsome large, covered, cut-glass bowl. The workmanship is choice and the patterns identical on both bowl and cover, yet the shade of glass in the two pieces is markedly different. Probably made from two different batches of the metal. In the making of this old glass the scum rose to the top and had to be skimmed off. The goods made from the glass in the top of the pot were known as "tale" goods and were inferior to those made from the glass in the middle of the pot, which was the best.

Few trades were more harassed by taxes than glass-making. In England a terrible excise duty was imposed in 1746 and so many and vexatious were the restrictions that it is a wonder that the industry survived. It was 1825 before the excise duty was introduced into Ireland, where there were flourishing glass-works at Cork, Belfast, Dublin and Waterford. The duty was imposed upon the molten glass in the crucible, "metal" it is called, and on unfinished goods. So as soon as the glass-maker got these out of the clutches of the excise man he set to work to decorate his glass as much as possible, so as to sell it at a sufficient profit to make it worth while.

The period between 1780 and 1810 is said to be the most important in English glass-making. It lasted about fifteen years longer in Ireland. It took, however, only twenty-five years of this excise duty on glass in the crucible and unfinished, to completely ruin the Irish branch of the industry, which has never been revived.

WATERFORD GLASS

T HE making of glass in the city of Waterford was
begun in 1729. The factory—there was only
one—closed in 1851. Mr. Westropp says that
between 1740 and 1783 no glass was made in or near
Waterford.

Joseph Harris was the first manufacturer to set up
a glass-house at Waterford, and later in the century,
1783, George and William Penrose established a glass-
house and made much glass. They sold their works,
however, in 1799 to James Ramsey, Jonathan Gatchell
and Ambrose Barcroft. These men, under the firm
name of Ramsey, Gatchell and Barcroft, did business
together till 1811 when Jonathan Gatchell became sole
owner.

He continued the business till 1823, when the firm
of Gatchell and Walpole was formed. Jonathan Gatchell died this year, but the firm continued, and was
finally dissolved in 1835. From 1835 to 1848 the firm
name was George Gatchell and Co. In 1851 the factory was closed.*

Some idea of the amount of the output may be gathered when it is known that as many as two hundred

* Westropp: "Irish Glass."

workmen were daily at work at the glass-house up to 1820 and that an equal number had been employed for thirty-six years.*

But the most interesting point, to Americans at least, is that thousands, hundreds of thousands of pieces of this glass were sent to the United States, that Gatchell's account books duly set it down and that American newspapers advertised it for sale. As late as 1842 George Gatchell and Co. announced that they made "every article made of glass for use, luxury or adornment; also chandeliers, lustres, lamps, hall bells, and candelabra in bronze, ormolu and glass. Medical establishments supplied."

Prior to 1795 that splendid old potter, Wedgwood, combined his beautiful blue and white ware in candelabra with glass for branches and prisms. They are very rare in this country, but in October, 1921, two pairs were sold at auction in New York City. They were listed as "Waterford glass candelabra with Wedgwood bases." One pair brought five hundred dollars, the other five hundred and ten dollars.

Through the courtesy of *Antiques* one of these candelabra is shown in Figure 74. Most of these candelabra have crystal chains, but these chains are crystal and blue glass Amber glass was also occasionally used. A pair of candelabra somewhat similar, and which belonged to General Washington, are on

* *Waterford Mirror*, May 5, 1820.
*Figure 74, page 159.*

exhibition at the Smithsonian Museum at Washington. They are extremely beautiful and quite perfect.

This Waterford glass is no more perishable than the old Staffordshire bone paste crockery which was hunted out in such quantities some years ago. Indeed, when you come to special pieces, that is aside from drinking glasses and bottles, more care was taken of them than of the crockery. After the making of flint glass was established the glass improved in quality and the cutting of glass after 1740 was quite general.

By 1786 Waterford was sending large quantities of assorted glass to New York. In 1793 they sent there 36,000 drinking bottles, and two hundred and ninety pounds' worth of other glassware. From 1796 to 1798 Waterford sent to New York 100,382 drinking glasses, and three hundred and seventy-five pounds' worth of other glassware. Nor was New England left without her quota, for in 1805, 17,280 drinking glasses and five hundred and forty-five pounds' worth of other glassware were sent there. In 1811 New England absorbed 67,792 drinking glasses and four hundred and thirty-six pounds' worth of other glass.

Up to 1822 quantities of glassware, thousands and thousands of pounds' worth, were sent to this country, but after that date the amount declined. Mr. Westropp, speaking of the export trade, quotes letters showing that in 1819 many thousands of pounds' worth of Irish glass was sold in "Charlestown," Philadelphia, New York, Halifax, Newfoundland and Quebec.

There were manufactured at Waterford, baskets, butter coolers, cans, candlesticks, cruets, cream ewers, decanters, dishes, egg cups, jelly glasses, mustards, pickle jars, salts, bowls of many kinds, smelling bottles, sugar basins, squares, tumblers, wines and rummers, celery glasses and jugs, in addition to immense numbers of drinking bottles and many kinds of lighting fixtures.

One of the objects of the late eighteenth and early nineteenth centuries which is most frequently to be found is the decanter. They were kept with more care and not subjected to such rough usage as the domestic pieces and so escaped the breakage to which the latter are liable. These early decanters are most interesting. They come under the head of human documents, and they depict very clearly the manners and customs of the times. The necks are ringed, the bodies globular, and the stoppers are often very decorative. But it is these rings which make the decanters interesting. There may be one, two or three of these rings, generally with spaces between, so that fingers which were none too steady could get a good grip and not drop the decanter.

These rings were of different designs, plain rounded, cut in diamonds, triangular cut, square cut, feathered, double or triple. While the shapes of the bodies of the decanters varied somewhat as the years went by, those of the early nineteenth century still maintained their ribbed necks. One of these decanters of Waterford glass is shown in Figure 75. It is owned by the Victoria and Albert Museum, London, and is the only specimen of old Irish glass which they own which they know definitely to be Waterford. It is marked "Penrose" on the base.

There was much glass made to order at Waterford for the old Irish families. More pieces than were needed to fill an order were blown, so that it would be on hand to fill breakages or enlarge sets. That accounts for the fact that in England and in Ireland many pieces of this ancient glass are found entirely undecorated.

While experts will not admit that Waterford glass had a bluish tint, it is true that they were constantly striving to improve the colour. In 1832 Elizabeth Walpole, one of the partners in the Waterford glassworks, says with reference to some glass she was sending over from Waterford for sale, that a glass merchant of Plymouth had told her that all the Irish glass he had ever seen was dark coloured, "but she told him she had sent for some Waterford glass so that he might see for himself." This letter is quoted in Mr. Westropp's book, "Irish Glass."

There are certain characteristics which are found on known Waterford glass, so that we think that at last we have something definite, when lo, the same thing turns up on some other factories' work, which may be

*Figure 75, page 160.*

Fig. 83.  BOWL AND BASIN AND TUMBLER

Fig. 85.  CORK DECANTERS

(*See pages* 198 *and* 200)

(*See page* 199)

Fig. 84.  CORK DECANTER

Fig. 86.  CUT GLASS, CORK
Fig. 87.  CUT GLASS, CORK

(*See page* 200)

Fig. 88. MOULDED GLASS, DUBLIN

Fig. 90. GOBLET, DUBLIN
Reverse.

Fig. 89. GOBLET, DUBLIN

(*See page* 203)

Fig. 91. THREE WISTARBERG PITCHERS AND WISTARBERG VASE
(*See page* 214)

Fig. 92. FOUR EXAMPLES OF DOUBLE-DIPPED GLASS
(*See page* 215)

Fig. 94. BROWN WISTARBERG PITCHER

THE METROPOLITAN MUSEUM OF ART

Fig. 93. AMBER BOWL AND BALL

(*See page* 215)

marked. Many of the pictures which are used to illustrate this chapter on Irish glass came from the National Museum, Dublin. All of them were labelled by the director himself. In Figure 76 two jugs are shown. They are labelled "probably Waterford, about 1820-30." As a rule this old glass is very heavy, it had to be when the cutting was to be deep. The edges of the articles were seldom plain, but were scalloped, saw-toothed, either large or small, fan-shaped or castellated. These jugs are most typical, the one on the right showing what is known as "lustre" cutting, that one on the left showing what we call "thumb-spots," but what the Irish or English glass-worker called "printies." This jug also has step cutting on the neck. But alas for calling the one with the lustre cutting definitely Waterford. In that device on the membership card of the Cork Glass Cutter's Society already mentioned, there is used as the central decoration an exact replica of this jug.

Mrs. Graydon Stannus in her book, "Old Irish Glass," says that "much cutting on the glass ware was done outside the glass-houses by men who had cutting sheds in their own homes, which accounts for the individuality of the work done."

Figure 77, also labelled "probably Waterford, 1820-30," shows an unusual plain edged piece. The bowl has a rayed cutting underneath the foot, a splendid fan-shaped edge and the strawberry cutting within the dia-

*Figures 76 and 77, pages 161 and 162.*

monds, so often confused with hob-nail. The celery glass is heavily cut, showing that it is of the later period, for the early specimens are so lightly cut that it is hardly more than heavy engraving. One of the examples in Figure 78 speaks for itself, a charming little scent bottle; and the toilet bottles show variations of popular diamond cutting. These are Waterford also, and like the scent bottles are of very clear white glass.

The tumblers of the early nineteenth century had most generous proportions, like those of an earlier period, and the same decorations. In Figure 79 the smallest one on the left is marked "probably Waterford," and the other two "probably Cork." But the swag and line cutting on the middle one was very much used at Waterford, and there are large services of glass held in both England and Ireland, known to have come from Waterford, which have exactly the same cutting.

The decoration above the diamonds on the Waterford tumbler is known as "blazes," they may be slanting like these or straight up and down. I have a number of tumblers, and smaller glasses for liquor, with flutes at the bottom and blazes above. They are the remnants of a set which have come to me by inheritance, and which I satisfy myself by calling Irish glass.

In the Pennsylvania Museum, Philadelphia, are the interesting pieces shown in Figure 80. The director, Mr. Samuel Woodhouse, Jr., is rather inclined to follow the example of the director of the Dublin Museum, and call them "probably Waterford." The tall glasses

*Figures 78, 79 and 80, pages 163 and 164.*

with domed foot and knopped stem are unusual, but stems like these are seen on many of the candle and taper sticks which were made in such quantities at Waterford. The decanter with its step and diamond cutting and ornamental stopper, combines two of the most popular Waterford decorations. Not only candlesticks, but wall-lights, candelabra and chandeliers were made both on private order and kept in stock for many years, at Waterford.

Mrs. Stannus says in her book, "Old Irish Glass," that a peculiarity of the Waterford glass drops was their oval shape. These drops appeared on many of the lighting fixtures which were made in infinite variety. They were for one candle or many, with drops or without, with arms or hand-bent branches, with stars or spear-heads or even crescents on top as ornaments. Some of the chandeliers were eight feet long and weighed over two hundred pounds, being formed on iron rods covered with silvered tubing.

General Washington, always eager to adorn and beautify his home, had many of these beautiful lighting fixtures. Besides those on exhibition at the Smithsonian Museum, are others hanging on the walls at Mount Vernon. There must be others stowed away somewhere in this country.

In handling this old glass it is remarkable to note how pieces which have come down in families as "sets" vary in colour. A pair of jugs, very beautifully cut with diamond and step cutting, with a pinched lip and rayed base, which belong to me, are absolutely different in colour. One of them is steely blue but the other is quite yellowish. These heavy glass jugs had three or four cuts in the top of the handle to prevent the thumb from slipping, and the handles were very thick and solid, quite different from the handles of early American glass.

On the eighteenth century Waterford glass very little engraving or gilding is found. The engraving was done by itinerant journeymen who went about the country carrying the little copper wheels which they used in this work, arranged in a small box, the motive power being supplied by a small boy who turned a handle which drove a shaft and two wheels which were inside the box.*

The best gilding was done by a man named Grahl, about 1786, and it is said to have the merit of resisting wear, and cannot easily be scraped off.

Mrs. Stannus, whose immense collection of Irish glass, particularly Waterford, has come to her through inheritance and by pati nt search, deplores the increasing number of fakes. These are not only modern but date back to those days when Irish glass became so much sought for domestic use. The modern reproductions come from France, Germany, Belgium and Holland, and some very recent ones from Bohemia. But these latter betray their origin by showing a pinkish tinge.

* Stannus: "Old Irish Glass."

## DUBLIN AND CORK GLASS

GLASS-WORKS were early established in Dublin and glass-making became an important industry early in the eighteenth century. The name of the first manufacturer as given by Mr. Westropp was Captain Philip Roche, who established his glass-works about 1690, and carried on the business till 1713 when he died. The Fitzsimons family which was associated with him in the glass-works carried on the business till 1787, when the firm became bankrupt.

This glass-house, known as the Round Glass House, was an important one. It advertised its wares freely, as may be seen from the following, taken from *Faulkner's Dublin Journal,* January, 1752:

"At the Round Glass House on George's Hill, near Mary's Lane, Dublin, are made and making all sorts of the newest fashioned drinking glasses, water bottles, claret and Burgundy ditto, decanters, jugs, water glasses with and without feet and saucers, plain, ribbed, and diamond moulded jelly glasses of all sorts and sizes, sillybub glasses, comfit and sweetmeat glasses, orange glasses, bells and shades, hall lanthorns for one to four candles, glass branches, cut and plain barrel lanthorns, globe lamps, etc., all in the most elegant and newest fashioned mounting now used in London; chamber ditto; all sorts of apothecaries' bottles, spaecia glasses of all sizes, rounds, urinals, breast and sucking bottles, cupping glasses, funnels, etc. All sorts of tubes, globes, etc., for electrical experiments, weather glasses, receivers for air pumps, and all sorts of philosophical experiments. All sorts of cut and flowered glasses may be had of any kind to any pattern, viz: wine glasses with a vine border, toasts or any flourish whatsoever; beer ditto with the same, salts with or without feet, sweetmeat glasses and stands, cruits for silver and other frames all in squares and diamond cut, gardevins, tea cannisters, jars and beakers for mock china, mustard pots, crests and coats of arms, sweetmeat bowls and civers, etc. N. B. As no pains or expense have been spared by the proprietor to procure the best workmen and patterns from London, he hereby hopes (that as his is the only manufacture of glass in the Kingdom, and that he is determined by his own personal inspection and application to support it in the highest perfection) to deserve the encouragement and approbation of all who shall honour him with their commands, and further promises them the greatest satisfaction in regard to colour and workmanship, beside the advantage of purchasing the above at much cheaper rates from him than those imported from England or elsewhere to be sold. Constant attendance will be given from eight o'clock in the morning until 9 o'clock at night at the glass warehouse on George's Hill."

There were a number of other glass-houses established in Dublin from time to time, the most important of which was that opened by Richard Williams and Co. in May, 1771. They advertised that they made "glass lustres, girandoles, chandeliers, candlesticks and candle moulds, pyramids, salvers, bowls, decanters, wafer dishes, drinking glasses and smelling bottles and every other article that can be made of flint glass, cut, engraved and plain." They also made plate glass for looking-glasses, windows and coaches. Various members of the family carried on the business till June, 1827, when the last member of the firm died.

In Figure 81 is shown a claret jug, of either Dublin or Cork manufacture, and of the late eighteenth century period. It is decorated with strawberry diamond cutting separated with bars. There is also the

*Figure 81, page 165.*

favourite leaf design, and heavily domed foot. The turnover bowl with feet is an unusual specimen. It is called "Dublin or Cork" and is of late eighteenth century. The turnover is richly cut, and on the bowl itself is a band of printies, in oval form.

In Figure 82 the piece on the right is "probably Cork," and the one on the left "probably Dublin or Cork." The one on the left is of peculiar interest to me. It is of the much desired boat shape, is lightly cut with the famous old leaf design of the eighteenth century, and has the cut base which is so much admired. The edge has a gracefully castellated scallop, and a heavy diamond cut on each side gives variety to the leaf design. I have one like it, an heirloom, which can be traced to the first quarter of the nineteenth century, but which probably is older. The other bowl with heavy turnover edge is of a shape made in every Irish glass-works. Indeed it has become the practise, in Great Britain at least, to call such Irish glass as cannot be distinguished as belonging to any particular glass-works as "Munster." This covers the output from Waterford, Cork, and to a certain extent Belfast. It should include Dublin too, but it is sometimes claimed that old Dublin glass has an unmistakable tint, quite yellowish in tone, which Waterford and Cork never had.

Irish glass is very tough, it sings with a clear note when struck, and Mrs. Stannus claims for it a softness to the touch entirely lacking in English glass of the

*Figure 82, page 166.*

same period. All glass of a good quality emits a clear note when struck, modern as well as ancient, so it does not seem that one can use this as a test of old glass.

The presence of minute air bubbles is common, you will find them in many pieces, but they are far less observable in the Irish glass than they are in the English glass, particularly of the same period.

The last makers of flint glass in Ireland were the brothers Thomas and John Pugh. They established works in Dublin about 1852. Thomas and his son Richard took over the works in 1863, and after the death of his father, Richard carried on the business till 1895, when the manufacture of flint glass in Ireland ceased.*

Besides the white flint glass they made quantities of coloured glass, amber, purple, blue and green. The bowl and basin and tumbler shown in Figure 83 are very heavy cut-glass pieces. The diamond cutting on bowl and basin is deep and the bars between wide and cut in flutes. The tumbler has both step cutting and panels, and is marked "probably Waterford, early nineteenth century." The bowl and basin are late eighteenth or early nineteenth century.

The Cork Glass House had goods on sale in February, 1785, and ten years later were advertising that they could fill all orders for flint glass with accuracy and despatch. Before the Cork Glass House finally

* Westropp: "Irish Glass."
*Figure 83, page 183.*

ceased work in 1818, a new one called the Waterloo
Glass House was opened. The proprietor evidently
fancied starting off with a flourish, for he put the following advertisement in the *Overseer,* a Cork weekly
newspaper, on December 24, 1816:

> "Waterloo Glass House. By his forming the Waterloo Glass
> House Company, which is now at work, Mr. Daniel Foley is giving
> employment to more than one hundred persons. His workmen are
> well selected, from whose superior skill the most beautiful glass
> will shortly make its appearance to dazzle the eyes of the public,
> and to outshine that of any other competitor. He is to treat his
> men at Christmas with a whole roasted ox, and with everything
> adequate. They have a new band of music with glass instruments,
> bessons serpents, horns, trumpets, etc., and they will have a glass
> pleasure boat, a cot and a glass net, which when seen will astonish
> the world."

The Waterloo Glass Works ceased work in 1835,
and all the fittings and materials were sold off, including a large quantity of richly cut glass, and the contents
of a dwelling house, presumably that of the owner of
the works.

The Terrace Glass Works was opened in 1818, but
like all the other glass-works could not stand up against
the taxes and other restrictions, and finally was closed
in 1841. With this closing the making of glass ceased
in Cork, having lasted nearly sixty years. Figure 84
shows a moulded decanter. It is one of the few specimens which form an oasis of safety for the glass collector who wishes that other firms had pursued the same
method. This decanter is marked on the base, "Cork

*Figure 84, page 184.*

Glass Co." The two decanters in Figure 85 are also marked, the one with the stopper, "Waterloo Co. Cork," and the other one, also marked on the base, "Cork Glass Co." This latter one was made about 1810, the other one about ten years later.

Three cut-glass jugs are shown in Figure 86, all of which are probably Cork, early nineteenth century. The centre one is decorated with wide shallow diamonds which are rather unusual, the diamond cutting on the jug to the right being a commoner size. There is step cutting on the neck and lip, and a pointed edge. The handle has a thumb-hold instead of the several small cuts which the glass-maker so often made use of. But it is not a pretty jug, heavy and clumsy, the upper part looking far too large for the body. The other two are more admirable in every way, the one on the left being an extremely popular pattern in both English and Irish glass-works. It was copied in moulded glass in America, and later in cut glass.

The effects of the excise law which taxed metal in uncut state is visible in the two pieces in Figure 87. The sweetmeat jar and stand and the celery glass are decorated to death, for only by excessive cutting so a high price could be asked was it possible for the glass-worker to make any profit. These pieces are ascribed to Cork and the early nineteenth century. It was not long after these were made that glass-making in Ireland practically ceased.

*Figures 85, 86 and 87, pages 183 and 185.*

The old Irish cut-glass is so much in demand by collectors that the charm of moulded glass is practically overlooked. Decanters have already been shown, and in Figure 88 is a pair of moulded glass butter coolers. These are marked "Francis Collins, Dublin," and were probably a late output of these works.

Occasionally butter coolers, sugar basins and finger bowls are found of a wonderful shade of rich green glass. They are decorated with simple panels or flutes, the splendid colour being all that is necessary.

After many of the Irish glass-works were closed, as in the case of those in England, the stranded glass-workers tried to eke out a living by making and selling small objects in glass. Sometimes these were freak things, toys and canes, but more often they were small drinking glasses or articles for domestic use. The quality of the glass was poor, greenish in colour and filled with bubbles.

Glass was also made in Newry, Ballycastle and Londonderry, but only in small quantities and for short periods of time. In his book on "Irish Glass" Mr. Westropp says he has been shown specimens said to have been made at Newry, but as there was nothing to prove it he let it go at that. Even less is known of what was made at Ballycastle and Londonderry, probably only black bottles.

From 1825 the glass trade in Ireland began to decline, and by 1845 most of the glass-houses had ceased

*Figure 88, page 186.*

working and those that still remained open had greatly decreased their output. The fact that such quantities of Irish glass were sent to various sections of America has impressed experts in Europe. Mr. Westropp states that it is quite possible that there is more old Irish glass here than there is in Ireland.

To bear out this contention Mr. Westropp quotes from the Custom House books which are preserved in the National Library of Ireland, regarding the glass sent to various places in this country. As early as 1781 glass in quantity was exported from Ireland. In the year 1784 Cork and Dublin sent to Quebec, Pennsylvania, Newfoundland, the Barbadoes and Carolina, 18,336 drinking glasses.

In 1791, 64,348 drinking glasses were sent to New York, New England, Carolina, Pennsylvania, Virginia, Maryland, Newfoundland and the Barbadoes, by Dublin, Waterford, Belfast, Cork, Londonderry and Newry. They also sent about twenty thousand vials, and what was more important still, they sent almost two thousand pounds' worth of other glassware. This sum would cover a large amount of glass at the prices of those days.

So it went on year after year; in 1802 Waterford sent to Pennsylvania and Virginia alone 130,740 drinking glasses. In fact it is perfectly amazing to realise what enormous quantities of this Irish glass which is so eagerly sought came to this country. Surely it cannot all be broken!

Between 1805 and 1812 hundreds of thousands of drinking glasses were sent to New York, New England and the Southern states from Waterford, Cork, Dublin and Belfast. After that date the number of drinking glasses declined, but the value of other glassware increased, so that in the next ten years more than one hundred and thirty-two thousand pounds' worth of glassware other than drinking glasses and bottles were sent to America.

With regard to the bluish tint which is so often ascribed to Waterford, both Mr. Westropp and Mrs. Stannus are agreed. He says: "I would wish now, once for all, to state that the glass made in Waterford has not the blue or dark tint always ascribed to it. . . . Dublin and especially Cork glass often has the blue or dark tint. I have never seen a marked Waterford piece with the blue tint."

Too early dates are often ascribed to Irish glass, for Waterford, Cork, Belfast and some of the Dublin works only operated about twenty years of the eighteenth century, while the largest output was during the nineteenth century.

The goblet shown in Figures 89 and 90 was made by the Pughs about 1870 for an Orange Lodge. It is said that they employed four Germans to do their engraving.

*Figures 89 and 90, page 187.*

# PART II

Fig. 90½.  BLUE STIEGEL, BUSWELL COLLECTION

WITH the multiplication of articles to make the business of living easier, it is hard to realise how the first settlers in this country got along at all. To my mind one of the most wonderful things of all is the way the Pilgrim Mothers settled down to their work and apparently made no complaints. At least none have come down in the records which detail so many of the small happenings which befell the pioneers.

The early drinking vessels must have been pewter, wood or leather mugs or jugs. They worried along somehow with these things till there were sales of fish and masts; till the apple orchards began to come in bearing, till the cattle increased, and they could draw breath from tilling the fields and fighting the Indians, and consider providing the comforts of a home.

While Caspar Lehmann was experimenting in Bohemia, the New World was trying to establish a glassworks in the infant colony at Jamestown, Va.; 1607 is the date given for the erection of this first furnace, and bottles only were made, so these are the oldest branch of the industry in this country.

In 1620 a subscription list was started in Jamestown to erect a factory for the manufacture of beads for trade with the Indians, and in 1621 the London Company sent Italian workmen to make them.*

This plant, which was situated some distance from Jamestown, escaped the massacre of 1622, and is heard of as late as 1623.

No further attempt was made in Virginia, apparently. But the need was urgent. When glass-making was seriously attempted in America has not been definitely settled. All authorities agree, however, that Salem, Massachusetts, was early in the field. Weeden, in his "Economic History of New England," says these glass-works were opened in 1638.

This business at Salem grew beyond its original capacity, and the court gave official sanction to the industry by ordering a loan. In 1640 Salem was authorised to lend the glass men thirty pounds and deduct it from the next rate laid on the town. These works were operated with more or less success for more than thirty years, and were finally closed in 1670 for "lack of capital."

Jan Smeedes in 1654 and Evert Duyckingk in 1655 were glass-making rivals in New Amsterdam, in what was originally called "Glass-Maker's Street," but is now known as William Street, New York. But what these rival glass-makers did at their glass-houses cannot be set down. Perhaps they found the barter of pelts

*Records of the Virginia Company in London.

or schnapps more profitable. At any rate no more is heard of their efforts.

Though mention of glass-making is made in Pennsylvania, in a letter written by William Penn in 1683, he does not state where.

Window glass, which we use so freely to-day that we hardly think about it, was one of the acute needs of the early colonists. In Virginia where there were earliest any houses which made any pretensions to comfort, there were few which had glass in the windows. Oiled paper and sliding wooden panels were the usual substitutes. In June, 1684, Colonel William Byrd, one of the original F. F. V.'s, sent to his agent in London for 400 feet of glass with drawn lead and solder in proportion. This glass was for use in his first house, Belvidere, for he did not begin the building of the famous Westover till 1688.

At these early glass factories in America where window glass was the chief product, there were almost always some bottles blown for the use of the workers if not for sale. The corner pots where odds and ends of metal were thrown, provided the material, and the rule was general that the glass-workers could use it free of charge. Quantities of specimens which their owners assign to definite factories were no doubt made at some of these glass-works where the regular product was window glass or common glass bottles, and the workmen used their privilege and made for their own use or for sale such pieces as pleased their fancy.

Like their European brothers in the trade, the glass-workers were a roving lot, travelling from one place to another, carrying their technique with them, and copying patterns that they were familiar with and liked. They were of many nationalities, so that it is no wonder that early American glass follows closely what was current at the same time in Europe.

IN 1739, Caspar Wistar, a Philadelphia merchant whose original business was making brass buttons, turned his attention to glass-making and began to construct a plant in Salem County, New Jersey, which was afterward known as Wistarberg, and sometimes as Allowaystown.

Frederick W. Hunter states in his book, "Stiegel Glass," that this glass-works of Wistar's was the first successful glass industry in America.

Caspar Wistar landed in Philadelphia in 1717, twenty-one years old, with not much money, but a capacity for making it in whatever enterprise he attempted. Wistar imported from Holland glass-makers to work in his factory, and the Dutch influence is clearly discernible not only in the early output, but in the later work. These Dutch artisans were contracted to teach the art of glass-making to Caspar Wistar and his son Richard, and to no one else. The factory began operations late in 1739.

They made window glass in five sizes, many kinds of bottles, lamp chimneys, snuff and mustard bottles, "electrofying globes and tubes," bowls, dishes, pitchers, canisters, preserve jars, sweetmeat bottles and drinking glasses. The first output was of plain glass, chiefly window glass and bottles, but later they excelled in making many objects of great beauty both as to form and colour. In Figure 91 are shown three pitchers and a vase of Wistarberg make. They display the characteristic two-coloured work in which this factory excelled, the darkest pitcher of all being extremely brilliant, with a ruby ground and pale green wavings. The one with the pinched base is perhaps the earliest though it may have been just the fancy of the individual workman. This group is at the Metropolitan Museum of Art, New York.

Mr. Hunter gives to Wistar the credit of being the first maker of flint glass in this country, and also gives him the precedence over all other manufacturers for using both clear and coloured glass in one object, sometimes indeed two or three in whorled and artistic patterns.

The dark blue glass which may or may not be attractive to the eye, owing to the richness of shade, was made at Wistarberg in small quantities only. They used instead a lighter, more delicate shade, turquoise almost, from which were fashioned many lovely objects. They made opalescent glass, clear green, very beautiful in all its shades, amber, and rarest of all brown. To my taste the most exquisite of their output is a soft shade of yellow with shifting turquoise lights in it, and used only for delicate and dainty objects. There is a scent bottle of it at the Smithsonian Museum

*Figure 91, page 188.*

which belonged to Martha Washington. I have recently seen a similar one on sale, and Leslie Buswell's splendid collection of American glass at Gloucester, Massachusetts, is rich in it.

The method of making the two-coloured, or double-dipped, glass was as follows: A partially completed object of one colour was decorated with whorls or lines of another in floral designs or the effects of breaking waves, the same pattern being carried out on the covers to match. Four examples of this decorative treatment are shown in Figure 92. They are at the Metropolitan Museum.

Bowls of many sizes, and bottles, some of these latter with handles, were put out in large numbers by the Wistarberg factory. Much of this product was in the favourite green glass, sometimes very charmingly whorled with white, not so delicate but in the same style as Nailsea glass.

At Wistarberg they had a way of blowing balls of glass, matching and to be used as covers for their bowls and pitchers. The anti-germ idea was struggling for birth even then. These balls ranged in size from those a foot in diameter made to cover large bowls, to those scarcely larger than marbles to fit the tiny creamers. Figure 93 shows such a bowl and ball, in amber glass.

What is probably the choicest piece of Wistarberg now extant is shown in Figure 94. It is a dark amber, rarest of all Wistarberg colours, with lily-pad design

*Figures 92, 93 and 94, pages 189 and 190.*

and spiral glass thread around the flaring neck. It is nine inches high, six inches in diameter, and was bought at the Herbert Lawton sale in 1923 by Mr. Buswell.

One of the prettiest little things which came from the Wistarberg works was the scent bottle, which was made in greatest variety of shape and colour. Some were small enough to slip into a glove, and no doubt took the place of the apple stuck full of cloves which Colonial belles were used to carry. These bottles are made in clear or coloured glass, or in combinations of two or three colours, in various shapes, the oddest being the "sea horse" pattern shown in Figure 95. Some of the bottles are decorated with strips of crimped glass on the sides, others are in plain flask shape, but all are very dainty and desirable.

There is a constantly growing market for these pieces, and their admirers are many. While not so much in demand as the Stiegel glass there are plenty of collectors who pick up when possible these charming bits of artistic worth.

While it is true that the Wistarberg glass-works were in operation from 1759 to 1780, and put out large quantities of glass, it is also true that there were other glass-works in operation in that neighbourhood, but the factories were small and the output inconsiderable.

The Wistarberg works made much useful ware, like the mortar and pestle in clear and amber glass, shown in Figure 96, or the sweetmeat jar in Figure 97. The

*Figures 95, 96 and 97, page 225.*

green and amber cup, Figure 98, and the pale green candlestick in Figure 99, and the sturdy pitcher in Figure 100 are all pieces of interest and beauty. These are at the Metropolitan Museum of Art, New York.

In 1775 a factory was started at what is now known as Glassboro, by two of Wistar's workmen. Indeed this factory is still in operation under the name of the Whitney Glass Works, Glassboro, New Jersey.

While the general appearance of this Jersey glass has a strong family resemblance, such pieces as those shown in Figures 101, 102, 103 are without doubt from Wistarberg alone. Up to nearly the middle of the nineteenth century small factories for glass-making were started up in this neighbourhood and along the Mullica River. None of them were in operation very long, nor is the product easily distinguishable from that made in the neighbourhood.

Like the workmen in the great English potteries, they did not seem to strike roots, but wandered about from one glass-works to another as fancy dictated. What made the output from these factories still more similar is the fact that most of the factories were started and carried on by men trained in the Wistarberg works, or their descendants.

J. B. Kerfoot, writing a note upon this South Jersey glass, says: "Again and again, as a matter of proved and indisputable fact, three generations of these workmen continued for more than a hundred years to make

*Figures 98, 99, 100, 101, 102 and 103, pages 225, 226 and 227.*

for themselves and their friends the same range of pieces, unaltered in form and indistinguishable in technique. So that, so far as concerns these wholly true-to-tradition specimens, the attempt to differentiate between 'true Wistarberg' and South Jersey pieces is utterly futile and meaningless."

By 1850 a change of style seems to have taken place. The old forms vanished, new ideas with reference to colouring and decoration were put into practise and the charm of the earlier ware was lost, but Caspar Wistar's influence had lasted more than a century. At his death in 1752 he left the glass-works, its contents, etc., to his son Richard. The latter never lived at Wistarberg, but employed a manager, Benjamin Thompson, to run the works. They were carried on till about 1780, when the effects of the Revolution crippled all business. A hundred years later only a log house and a splendid sycamore-tree marked where once a flourishing factory stood by the side of the road.

No collector thinks his collection complete without one of the fine squat schnapp, gin or whiskey bottles which were made in such quantities at this time. The one shown in Figure 104 in a rich green, which is an unusual colour for these bottles, and adds to its beauty. They are commonly found in amber or a greenish brown.

One of the dainty little scent bottles which occasionally come to hand is given in Figure 105. I have one

*Figures 104 and 105, page 228.*

not so attractive in shape, but of a wonderful shade of dark blue.

Glass-works were opened at Millville, New Jersey, about 1820, and they turned out a great variety of objects. There were chains of glass, generally clear, glass lilies, paper-weights and glass balls to cover bowls and pitchers, Figure 106, though now they are generally called witch balls after the English style, and were said to have been made to hang in the window to ward off witches. They were often of great beauty, like the one shown in Figure 107 which is pink and white on a clear glass stand. This belongs to the Buswell collection.

*Figures 106 and 107, pages 228 and 229.*

THE story of the work of the early American glass-makers is still much fogged, except that of William Henry Stiegel which has been so exhaustively covered by the late Frederick William Hunter. His book, "Stiegel Glass," is inaccessible to most people, since an edition of 420 copies only was privately published, and the cost of such stray copies as come into the market is quite prohibitive.

In the preparation of his volume Mr. Hunter spared neither time, money nor himself, and the result is that the history of William Henry Stiegel has been traced from the time of his landing on these shores, August 31, 1750, at Philadelphia, to the date of his death at Charming Forge, January 10, 1785.

Briefly stated, William Henry Stiegel arrived in Philadelphia in 1750, at the age of twenty-one. On November 7, 1752, he married Elizabeth Huber, daughter of Jacob Huber, owner and operator of large iron furnaces in Lancaster County.

On September 22, 1756, with some men from Philadelphia he began the operation of the Huber iron furnace in Elizabeth township, Lancaster County, and here in 1763 he began experimenting with glass-making. He built two glass-houses at Manheim; the first one had the fire lighted under the pots on October 29, 1765. The output was chiefly bottles, ranging in size from a gallon to a pint; the smaller sizes were known as "pocket bottles"—see Figures 108 and 109. In Figure 110 are some very choice blue and amethyst bottles which belong to the Buswell collection. In addition to the bottles there were other articles listed under the head of "small glass"—see Figures 111, 112, 113, the latter a green glass milk bowl with blue rim, in the Buswell collection. On December 18, 1770, fire was lighted under the ovens of the second glass-house at Manheim, and glass of many kinds was made. In February, 1774, the sheriff sold the Manheim glass-houses and Stiegel's career as a business man was closed. So he was making glass just about ten years, a fact to be remembered by glass collectors.

Mr. Hunter was extremely fortunate in finding among the papers of John Dickinson, now in possession of the Pennsylvania Historical Society, a series of day books, journals and ledgers, relating to Elizabeth Furnace, Charming Forge and Manheim works. From these he was able to reconstruct the life story of William Henry Stiegel, which ended at the last in misery and wretchedness.

Although glass was made first at Elizabeth Furnace, Charming Forge was used only for the manufacture of bar iron and earned much of the money which was later used at Manheim. The first glass-house at Man-

Figures 108, 109, 110, 111, 112 and 113, pages 230, 231 and 232.

heim began work with about half a dozen blowers, and the product was sold to merchants in nearby towns.

The stamp act of 1765 had a depressing effect upon the business of the Colonies, and though it was repealed the next year, the Townshend act of 1767 levying duties on Colonial imports, bore heavily on crown plate, flint and white glass. But to Stiegel's mind this duty on imports should prove of great benefit to the industries of America.

An advertisement to this effect printed in the *Pennsylvania Journal and Weekly Advertiser,* July and August, 1769, shows his attempts to call the attention of the public to his wares. A beautiful arrangement of Stiegel glass, all clear, is shown in Figure 114. It is a part of Mr. Buswell's collection, all of which is arranged as a decoration to the rooms in which it is placed, rather than as a mere collection.

The variety of goods which Stiegel made may be judged from the following advertisements which appeared in the *Pennsylvania Gazette,* for June 27, 1771, and June 4, 1772. They are in the files of the Pennsylvania Historical Society, at Philadelphia.

### STIEGEL GLASS

This is to acquaint the public, and my kind customers in particular, I have lately been at the Glass Factory at Manheim, in Lancaster County, and contracted with Mr. William Henry Stiegel for a large and complete assortment of his Flint Glass, consisting of quart, pint, and half-pint decanters; pint, half-pint, gill and half-gill tumblers; wine glasses; vinegar glasses; salt-cellars; cream-pots;

*Figure 114, page 233.*

sugar dishes with covers; jelly glasses; syllabub glasses; proof
bottles; etc., etc.; to be delivered to me immediately at my house
in Market Street, next door to the Indian King, where I will sell
them as low or lower, and equal in quality with my flint glass
imported from England. Any orders shall be punctually complied
with, and be quickly forwarded, and will be exactly furnished from
the Manufactory.

Wanted. A Glass-Cutter and Grinder; such a workman by
applying will meet with good encouragement.

ALEXANDER BARTRAM.

Figure 115 from the Buswell collection and Figure
116 from the Metropolitan Museum, New York, show
some of the kinds of glass which Mr. Bartram could
furnish to his kind customers.

The following advertisement is even fuller in nam-
ing the different objects in glass which were being
made at the Manheim works.

### STIEGEL GLASS

#### Caullman & Fegan

To be sold, AMERICAN FLINT GLASS, greatly improved, and allowed by competent judges to be equal to the most improved from
England, is now to be sold wholesale and retail, at the American
Flint Glass store in Second Street, fifth door above Race Street,
by Caullman & Fegan, where they have just opened a large and
general assortment of the Manufactory, viz.

Double and single flint gallon, three quart, half gallon, and
single quart decanters with stoppers; sugar loaf ditto; round ditto;
single and double flint tumblers, pint measure, half pint ditto, and
gills; tall pint tumblers, pints and half pints; enamelled mason
wines; enamelled twisted mason wines; plain ditto, common wines;
twisted ditto, enamelled ditto; syllabubs, with one handle, ditto
with two handles; bubbled buttoned jellies; common acorn ditto;
jacony salts, and enamelled ditto; double and single cruets with
stoppers; tall, twisted and enamelled cruets; enamelled three footed
creams, common ditto; three footed salts, enamelled blue and plain;

*Figures 115, 116 and 117, pages 234, 235 and 236.*

inks of all sorts; and flower pots; garden pots; proof glasses; lemonade jars; candle-sticks, ornamented; servers, ornamented; common and enamelled mustards; vinegar and oil cruets, joined together; and great variety of glasses, too tedious to insert.

The public may rest assured that no other kind of glass will be kept, or sold in said store. From the great experience that the proprietor of this manufactory, Mr. William Henry Stiegel, has of the patriotic spirit of the Gentlemen in Pennsylvania, and the provinces adjacent, he flatters himself that it will meet with suitable encouragement. All orders of patrons sent to the store, shall be accurately forwarded and complied with, at the Manufactory, or at the Store, from time to time. All Store-keepers, Tavern-keepers, and Retailers, will be completely supplied to orders, lower than importation price.

That Stiegel possessed an optimistic disposition the financial records of his various business difficulties plainly show. He plunged into debt and yet more debt, and mortgaged everything available. He built himself a fine mansion at Manheim, and two tall towers, one at Elizabeth Furnace, another at Schaefferstown, on which cannon were placed. A third cannon graced the band platform on the top of the house at Manheim. His goings and comings were announced to the village by the cannon reports, and his coach, in which he rode from one place to another, served to accentuate his love of show, and no doubt had much to do with giving him his courtesy title of Baron.

He began at this time to advertise freely not only in the Philadelphia papers but in the *New York Gazette and Mercury*. On July 1, 1772, he adopted the name "The American Flint Glass Factory," and this, according to all records, was his most prosperous year.

Fig. 97.  SWEETMEAT JAR     Fig. 96.  MORTAR AND PESTLE

Fig. 99.  PALE GREEN CANDLESTICK

Fig. 95. SCENT BOTTLE           Fig. 98.  GREEN AND
                                         AMBER CUP

(See pages 216 and 217)

Fig. 100.  GROUP OF WISTARBERG

Fig. 101.  SOUTH JERSEY
PITCHER

Fig. 102.  SOUTH JERSEY
BOWL, BLUE

(*See page* 217)

Fig. 103.  SOUTH JERSEY VASES AND BOWL

(*See page* 217)

Fig. 104.  SOUTH JERSEY BOTTLE, GREEN

Fig. 105.  SOUTH JERSEY SCENT  Fig. 106.  MILVILLE, N. J., GLASS
BOTTLE                                           BALL

*(See pages 218 and 219)*

Fig. 107. GLASS BALL, BUSWELL COLLECTION
(*See page* 219)

Fig. 108.  STIEGEL POCKET BOTTLES, AMETHYST
Fig. 109.  STIEGEL POCKET BOTTLES

(*See page* 221)

Fig. 110.  BLUE AND AMETHYST BOTTLES
Fig. 111.  STIEGEL BOWL

(*See* *page* 221)

Fig. 112. STIEGEL BOWL WITH BLUE RIM
Fig. 113. STIEGEL JAR

(*See page* 221)

Fig. 114. CLEAR GLASS, STIEGEL

(See page 222)

Fig. 115. FOUR BLUE FLINT CREAM POTS

Fig. 116.  FOUR BLUE AND CLEAR GLASS CREAM POTS

(*See page* 223)

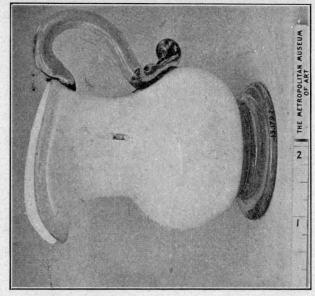

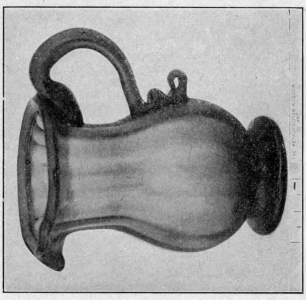

Fig. 117. EWER AND CREAM POT

(See page 223)

Fig. 118. BLUE FLINT SALT-CELLARS

(*See page* 241)

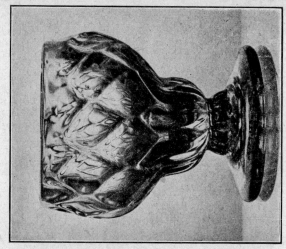

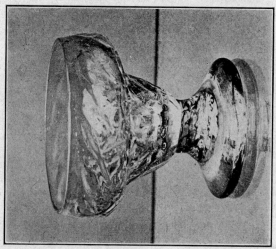

Fig. 119. CLEAR AND GREEN GLASS SALT-CELLARS

(*See page 241*)

Fig. 120. VINEGAR AND MUSTARD CRUETS

(*See page* 241)

Fig. 121.   BLUE FLINT SUGAR BOWLS
Fig. 122.   CLEAR GLASS SUGAR BOWL

(*See page* 242)

Among the "small glass" produced by Stiegel, his salts were particularly attractive. There were many shapes, and the blue flint ones, often in his best shade of blue, are more esteemed to-day than when he made them. Some of these in both blue and clear glass are shown in Figures 118 and 119.

Stiegel's glass was on sale at the store of Garret Rapelje, opposite the Fly Market in New York, and the venture must have been successful, since in January, 1773, he went to New York, rented a store on Broad Street, and advertised as follows in the *New York Journal or General Advertiser,* for January 14, and several weeks following:

### AMERICAN FLINT GLASS

#### *William Henry Stiegel*

Proprietor of the first American flint-glass manufactory in Pennsylvania, is just arrived in this city, and opened a warehouse near the Exchange, the corner opposite Mr. Waldron's, where he hopes for the encouragement of those who wish well to the establishment of manufacturers on this continent; and that the glass he offers to the public will be found to rival that which is imported, and sold at lower prices.

Quart, pint and half-pint decanters; pint crofts; double flint pint, half pint and jill tumblers; syllabub and jelly glasses; three-feeted salts and creams; wine and water glasses; vinegar and mustard cruets; phials and other bottles for Chymists and Apothecaries, etc.

As his stay in town will be very short, he begs the favor of an early application to him from those who want a supply of glassware.

Vinegar and mustard cruets are mentioned in this advertisement. Some are shown in Figure 120. The variety in sugar bowls is almost as great as in salts. A

*Figures 118, 119 and 120, pages 237, 238 and 239.*

number of these are shown in Figures 121, 122, 123, 124.

Stiegel did not retain the special warehouse very long, and is next heard of advertising from a new stand, in the months of February and March, 1773, in the *New York Gazette and Weekly Mercury*. James and Arthur Jarvis became his New York agents, and advertised on sale at their shop "between Burling and Beekman's Slip, in the Fly," an even greater assortment of goods than appeared in Stiegel's own advertisement. They had "of the American manufacture, quart, pint, and half pint decanters; pint, half pint, gill and half gill, flint and common tumblers; carrofts, enamel'd; mason, and common wine glasses; jelly and cillabub glasses, with and without handles; mustard and cream pots, flint and common; salts, salt-linings, and crewets; wide-mouthed bottles for sweetmeats, rounds and phyals for doctors, wine and water glasses, ink and pocket bottles. Orders taken for all kinds of glasses for chymical or other uses agreeable to order."

But with all his efforts and ceaseless activity things did not go well with William Henry Stiegel. His business affairs went from bad to worse, though in 1773-74 he organised lotteries to bolster up his fortunes. His credit was exhausted, the sheriff levied on his household goods, and finally in February, 1774, Manheim, the glass-house on which he had staked his all, was sold by the sheriff to George Ege, a nephew of Mrs.

*Figures 121, 122, 123 and 124, pages 240, 257 and 258.*

Stiegel. Ege soon became possessed of the entire property, built himself a fine house where later he took in and cared for Stiegel who had become an absolute bankrupt.

Indeed, for a few weeks he was imprisoned for debt, being liberated on Christmas day, 1774. This was a terrible blow for a man of Stiegel's temperament and position. The last years of this one-time prosperous and successful man were melancholy indeed. He was but fifty-six when he died, in January, 1785, and since his failure had eked out a poverty-stricken existence by teaching, giving music lessons, or giving any service which those living in that region might require.

In the heyday of Stiegel's prosperity he had deeded one of his Manheim lots, with a small church which he had built upon it and called the Zion Lutheran Church, to its board of trustees. It was quite a custom at this time when property was sold for a nominal cash consideration, to add also a nominal annual rent. Mr. Hunter says in "Stiegel Glass" that a peppercorn or a grain of wheat were favourite considerations. A red rose, which was the fee chosen by Stiegel, was, curiously enough, chosen also by Caspar Wistar to be paid in lieu of ground rent in many of his deeds. But the Wistar rose rent has faded into obscurity, while the red rose demanded by the Stiegel deed has blossomed into a ceremony which is observed the second Sunday in June at Manheim, which in its elaboration and picturesqueness would have given William Henry Stiegel abundant satisfaction. They call it the "Feast of the Roses," and for one day in the year Manheim emerges from the obscurity which enwraps it the other 364.

The collection of Stiegel which was gathered by Mr. Hunter and presented by him to the Metropolitan Museum, New York, covers the ground pretty thoroughly. It is so arranged that it can be conveniently studied by those who wish to add to their knowledge of this interesting and beautiful glass.

The illustrations given here are chiefly from this collection and that of Leslie Buswell at Gloucester, Massachusetts. In the Buswell collection are some pieces which are absolutely unique, like the splendid Stiegel cup which is the frontispiece of this book, and the large covered pitcher shown in Figure 134.

The first impression of the collection at the Metropolitan Museum, as a whole, is the comparatively small size of the objects. The pitchers are smaller than those we use at the present day, and few of them are as much as twelve inches tall. They have a certain fragility and delicacy which certainly would not stand the rough and tumble life of a modern dish-washer, human or mechanical.

A great number of the coloured pieces in the Hunter collection are blue, that splendid shade derived from the Bristol workmen who came here to make glass and teach the local workers the tricks of the trade. I have

Figure 134, page 267.

mentioned elsewhere what Mr. Hunter calls the "Bristol tradition" with reference to the colouring of Stiegel glass. But an acquaintance with Stiegel glass very soon teaches you that it is quite impossible to lay down rules as to what is "Stiegel blue." You can see for yourself in the Hunter or any other collection of Stiegel glass any number of shades in his blue flint, some of them rarely beautiful, some of them flat and verging on the indigo.

This variance of shade is nowhere more distinguishable than in the salt-cellars, many of which are besides delightfully crooked, one of the charms of hand-work.

Drinking glasses in numberless patterns and decorations were turned out at Manheim. The covered rummer in Figure 125 is an interesting piece, not only on account of the cover, but because of the panels of the glass itself. These panels are more often found on flip glasses and tumblers, and may be of equal size or alternating long and short. In the group of wine glasses shown in Figure 126 the one with the cotton twist stem is the most interesting. Both drawn and stuck stems were made at the Manheim works, and the method employed was the same as that in use at the English glass-works.

The next group is more decorative, Figure 127. These bowls are pattern moulded, and then expanded by blowing, or twisted by rolling on the arms of the glass-blower's chair, or by pinching with pucellas, as

*Figures 125, 126 and 127, pages 258, 259 and 260.*

in the diamond pattern. As a rule domestic wine glass feet are flatter than those of English make, and are more solid, and the edge of the foot is turned down and in, rather than up and over which is characteristic of English glasses.

Engraved glass made at the Stiegel works was done with the copper wheel and diamond method. Mr. Hunter distinguished fourteen types of design which were in use. The wine glasses in Figure 128 show four of these.

The flip glasses beloved of the deep drinker, and much sought by the modern collector, are generally very beautiful. The basket design holding flowers, and the tulip design, were most characteristically Dutch, copied from them by the English and then copied from both of them, over here. Four of these Stiegel engraved flips are shown in Figure 129. They are extremely attractive, the one with the panels in three lengths being particularly so. They seem too delicate to stand the hard usage to which flip glasses as a rule were subjected. Figure 130 shows some unusually fine engraved glasses, from the Buswell collection.

A charming pair of engraved jelly glasses is shown in Figure 131. They are rather tiny affairs, one and seven-eighths inches high, and three and a quarter inches in diameter. There is that pleasing irregularity in the

*Figures 128, 129, 130 and 131, pages 261, 262, 263 and 264.*

engraving which is indicative of hand-work, and the handles are similar but not identically alike.

It is not wonderful that with time and use, covers have parted company from the vessels they were made to go with. This group of covered flips, Figure 132, which belong to the Buswell collection are then all the more remarkable, and the one in the centre is the largest one known.

Stiegel made two shades of green; one, fine and clear and very brilliant, is seldom met with, while the other shade, far less attractive and quite pale, is more common. It depresses me to write about this pale green glass, for I lost a covered sugar bowl by hesitating over night to pay the price. There seems to be always somebody waiting to "snap up" these things, and she was on the spot while I was considering.

I have seen many pieces, particularly salt-cellars, in what might be called a smoky green. It looks as if they were made from odds and ends of metal from the corner pots, as no doubt they were. One such salt-cellar had several flecks of ruby red glass in it, not as decoration, but as part of the article itself. In fact this piece was given to me. I saw it at the house of a friend, tried to buy it from her, but she gave it to me saying, "You can have it, it only cost fifty cents, and I don't care for it."

If I had been as experienced in collecting old glass as I am now, I should have taken it then and there and

*Figure 132, page 265.*

borne it off in triumph. But I protested feebly at taking it as a gift, and went home. The next time I saw her she spoke of it and said she would send it. Here again I made a mistake. I should have gone for it. She arrived one snowy day with a shapeless parcel done up in tissue-paper. "Here is your salt-cellar," said she, "all that is left of it," and went on to say that she had given it to her chauffeur to deliver, but that as he had several other errands to do, somehow, in the course of his activities, he had sat upon it! There was nothing left but the base and stem, two or three bits, and some powdered glass. I tried later to impress the enormity of her carelessness upon her by showing her the record of an auction sale where a similar one had fetched $140.

Next to blue, purple ranging from a very rich bluish tone to a reddish amethyst seems to have been a popular product of the Stiegel factory. There was also amber, rarest of all, a warm tone and not very dark. Some of the very early bottles were in this warm brown. A very charming pocket flask with panels and daisy design is shown in Figure 133.

The variety of styles embodied in the various kinds of glass made at the Manheim works was owing to the different nationalities of the men employed there, English, Irish, German and Italian. At the new Manheim works nearly one hundred hands were employed and the choicest glass made. In addition to the moulded

*Figure 133, page 266.*

wares, there was the enamelled in German style, with clearer, brighter colours, and there was the etched and engraved which is now so eagerly sought by collectors.

Splendid pitchers with covers like the one shown in Figure 134 were occasionally made, either on order or for presentation pieces. This one belongs to the Buswell collection. Candlesticks like Figure 135 were also made, and more rarely vases, like the one in blue flint, which is given in Figure 136.

The struggle which Stiegel constantly maintained to produce goods as useful, beautiful and cheap as those which were constantly imported is more or less pathetic, when you consider his tragic end. Medicine glasses, Figure 137, egg cups, like the one in Figure 138, pitchers and compotes, Figure 139, and small decanters like the one given in Figure 140, were all parts of his regular output.

Mugs both in clear and coloured glass, with or without covers, plain or decorated, were made in numbers, and some are shown in Figure 141, two of blue flint and two of clear glass.

Of course the average collector can only hope to possess a few pieces of Stiegel glass. They are the gems of any collection. Such a piece as the flip, seven and a half inches high, clear glass, with the daisy-in-the-square design, Figure 142, or the amethyst bottle shown in Figure 133, is always at the back of my mind.

*Figures 134-142, pages 267-271.*

Some day I mean to own one or the other—my wildest dreams do not include both.

Panel pieces like the bowl in Figure 143 and the rummer in Figure 144 show the use of the panel as a decoration for otherwise plain pieces. But the last and probably in Stiegel's estimation the highest style of decoration attempted at the Manheim works was that in coloured enamels. The workmen who were employed to do this class of decoration were four in number, and the colours were fresher and brighter than the German colours, and the decoration was consequently more attractive. Mr. Hunter says six colours only were used. The two bottles in Figure 145 show how very effective this decoration may be.

There were designs which were used over and over again, like the steeple, Figure 146, the bird design, Figure 147, or the equally popular dove design shown on the mug in Figure 148. Less attractive than much of Stiegel's product, these too consciously follow foreign models to please the taste of those who like original work.

A cupboard of clear and coloured Stiegel glass which shows a portion of the Buswell collection is given in Figure 149. The pieces are charmingly arranged and are displayed against ground glass which is the true and proper background, particularly for coloured glass.

*Figures 143-149, pages 271, 272, 289 and 290.*

WITHIN the last few years many collections of early American glass have been sold. Though the pickings for the would-be collector are not what they were, there are chances still left.

In 1920 a collection made by Dr. Pleasant Hunter —what an ideal name for a collector—was sold at auction. The objects embraced in this sale were made in Pennsylvania, New Jersey, Massachusetts, Connecticut and New Hampshire. In a prefatory note to the catalogue, Dr. Hunter states that he gathered this collection, 862 pieces, in five years. That in January, 1913, and in November, 1915, he had disposed through the same hands of two previously made collections.

Without doubt the finest collection of early American glass which has ever been sold at auction was that gathered by Mr. Herbert Lawton of Boston, and sold in New York, February, 1923. Some of the choicest pieces of this collection are shown in this book through the courtesy of Mr. Buswell who bought them.

There were three hundred and forty-nine pieces in the Lawton sale, comprising all the finest products of American glass-works, and showing an unusual number of three-section mould pieces which are becoming increasingly interesting to the collector.

In the making of glass the most important necessity is an abundance of fuel near at hand. Western Pennsylvania and the neighbourhood of Pittsburg furnished this in quantity. The use of coal, and later of gas, still caused this section of the country to become important as a glass-making centre.

The first glass-works in Western Pennsylvania was started by Albert Gallatin in 1787, on the Monongahela River, about sixty miles above Pittsburg. In 1795 the first factory was built in Pittsburg itself, and both of these works made window glass only.

Mr. Isaac Craig, writing in 1880, says in his "Recollections" that the glass made at the early glass-houses was generally crude, and the "small wares" were made by the workmen from the corner pots. He writes, "I recollect distinctly seeing both tumblers and decanters made of green glass. In old times these decanters were used in every house, mostly by the poorer families who could not afford cut-glass. Whiskey was set out to every visitor in these decanters, and before and after every meal. Although of green glass they were not cut, but ornamented by beads around the neck."

O'Hara and Craig, General and Major in the Revolution, started in 1797 another plant on the Monongahela. Pittsburg has always retained its position in the glass-making industry, but it is within the last sixty years that the most important developments have taken place in the methods of making it.

The first glass factory to use coal was established at Pittsburg in 1797, but it was many years before it came into general use. Sand, one of the most important ingredients of glass, is found in abundance, and of superior quality, in America. Large deposits were found in Juniata County, Pennsylvania; Hancock County, West Virginia; Fox River, Illinois; Crystal City, Missouri; and Berkshire County, Massachusetts. When the war of 1812 cut off the supply of foreign sand, the sand from Plymouth Beach, Massachusetts, was used till better quality was discovered at Maurice River, New Jersey.

The superiority of this sand is attested by such experts as Thomas Webb and Son, of Stourbridge, England, who experimented with some sand from Massachusetts, and exhibited the result at London in 1851. Also by Bontemps, one of the greatest authorities on glass, and by Henry Chance of Birmingham, England, in his article, "On the Manufacture of Glass."

In the early factories window glass and bottle-making seemed to go together. It was not till after 1837 that factories were built exclusively for bottle-making.*

The glass-houses where flint glass was made, manufactured table and other ware, both blown and pressed. Pot metal is the term used for glass when the colour

*Tatum.

permeates the whole metal; flashed or double glass
when the colour is confined to the surface; and stained,
when it is burned in.

Bottle-making, one of America's first industries, became a very important one. Very necessary indeed
were bottles of every description. The fine old squat
ones, dark or light green or dark amber, are now much
in demand for decorative purposes. They have a delightfully raffish look and speak of those potations long
and deep in which our ancestors indulged. Three ven-
erable ones, assorted sizes, are shown in Figure 150.

There are occasionally to be found very charming
little decorative bottles like the one shown in Figure
151. It comes under the general heading "early American" where so much of this interesting and delightful
glass belongs, though the general tendency of collectors,
and dealers too, is to apply the name of some glass-
works to it without reference to facts.

C. A. Tatum in an article in the *Scientific American,*
entitled "One Hundred Years of Glass Achievement,"
has this to say on the subject of bottles:

"America is said to be the most wasteful country in
the world in the matter of bottles. It is not the custom
to save a bottle once it has served its purpose, particularly those which contain medicine. In Great Britain
and on the Continent it is the practice for those who
wish a prescription made up to furnish a well-washed
bottle which has served a similar use before. In fact

*Figures 150 and 151, page 291.*

an extra charge is made by the chemist if no bottle is furnished by the purchaser of the dose.

"At the beginning of the nineteenth century only two kinds of bottles were in general use for prescriptions or medicines. These were made of the commonest green glass, and were either long and slim like a phial, [Figure 152] or round and rather squat. The lip was thin and irregular in shape, making it difficult to drop liquid from it, so that the size of the drop continually varied. The drip from the bottle was so apt to destroy the label with directions that it was customary to tie this to the neck of a bottle with a string. The use of these bottles continued well into the century.

"Being so prodigal in the use of pharmacists' and other bottles it was fitting that America should make the first advances in bettering this form of glassware. About 1825 the octagon-shaped bottle made its appearance and was popular for a time, but was followed by the oval-shaped bottle as being more convenient.

"A heavier lip and a uniform shape to the mouth were found more adapted to prescription ware and were taken up by the trade. Tools were used instead of the old hand-work, and more regular results obtained.

"Then flint glass was substituted for the common green glass, the first of these appearing about 1861. Soon after a tall four-sided bottle with beveled edges was put on the market, and these 'French Squares,' as

Figure 152, page 292.

they were called, became very popular all over the country.

"About 1867 lettered bottles were made, sometimes with the whole name, monogram or some trade device, appearing in raised letters on the side. This was achieved by the use of a special device known as a plate mold which was made to fit the various molds used in casting bottles of different shape."

The various articles made in glass for lighting purposes were very numerous, including the many patterns of candlesticks and all kinds of lamps. In the latter were burned lard, tallow, common grease, and oil. The early lamps of the better class had two wicks instead of one, like the one shown in Figure 153. The font is of clear glass and the base of amber glass. It was often the fashion in those farmhouses where these lamps were cherished long after gas was in use in the cities, to put in the font a bit of red flannel. This was considered highly decorative, and certainly claimed attention.

The lamp in Figure 154 was made in Germantown, now Quincy, Massachusetts, and has a moulded font and a pressed base; it carries two wicks and belongs to the early nineteenth century.

The lamp given in Figure 155 is probably earlier than the two previous ones, about 1800. It is of clear glass with heavily knopped stem, domed base, and the

*Figures 153-155, pages 292 and 293.*

Fig. 123. BLUE AND CLEAR GLASS SUGAR BOWLS

(*See page* 242)

Fig. 125.  COVERED RUMMER
Fig. 124.  SUGAR BOWLS, STIEGEL
(*See pages* 245 *and* 242)

Fig. 126. WINE GLASSES WITH PLAIN BOWLS
(*See page* 245)

Fig. 127. WINE GLASSES WITH MOULDED BOWLS
(*See page* 245)

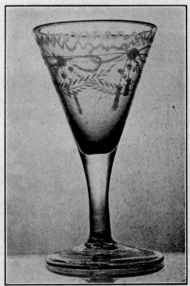

Fig. 128. WINE GLASSES WITH ENGRAVING

(*See page* 246)

Fig. 129. ENGRAVED FLIP GLASSES

(See page 246)

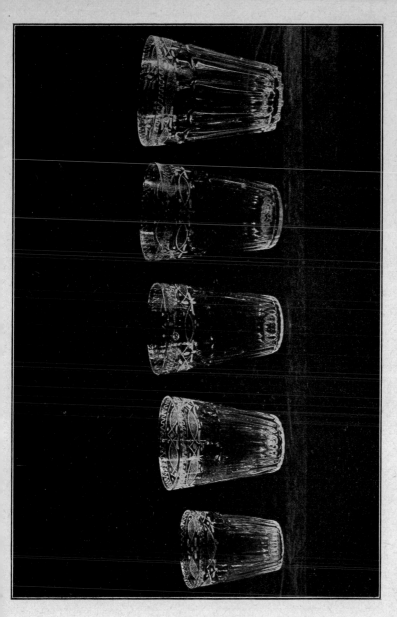

Fig. 130. ENGRAVED AND PANELLED GLASSES

(*See page 246*)

Fig. 131.  ENGRAVED JELLY GLASSES

(*See page* 246)

Fig. 132. COVERED FLIP GLASSES

(See page 247)

Fig. 133. BOTTLE WITH PANEL AND DAISY PATTERN
(*See page* 248)

Fig. 134. COVERED PITCHER

(See pages 244 and 249)

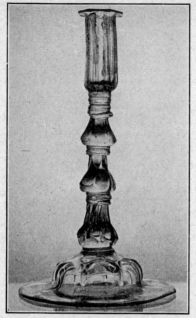

Fig. 135. CANDLESTICK

Fig. 137. MEDICINE GLASS

(*See page* 249)

Fig. 136. BLUE FLINT GLASS

Fig. 138. EGG CUP

Fig. 140. DECANTER
Fig. 139. BLUE PITCHERS AND COMPOTE

(*See page* 249)

(*See page* 249)
Fig. 141.  MUGS

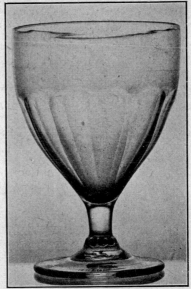

Fig. 143.  PANELLED BOWL

Fig. 142.  FLIP OF CLEAR
GLASS

Fig. 144.  RUMMER

(*See pages* 249 *and* 250)

Fig. 146.   STEEPLE DESIGN
Fig. 145.   ENAMELLED BOTTLES

(*See page* 250)

edge of the rim folded up and over, as was seen in the wine glasses of this period.

In 1815, Thomas Coffin, of Number Three, Chestnut Street, Philadelphia, announces in the *Daily Advertiser* that he has for sale:

Best winter-pressed spermaceti oil;
Second      do          do      do
Summer strained         do      do
Common & Humpback               do
Best Streights Liver            do
Second Quality   do             do

In the same issue of the paper appears the following notice:

*Great Sale of Elegant Lamps and Lustres, Store Lamps, etc.*
Will be sold at Public Auction, Monday morning next 27th. inst. at No. 4 South Third Street, an extensive and splendid collection of Lamps, Lustres, etc. And various articles appertaining thereto. Elegant Cut Glass Lamps for Mantles with one or two lights, ornamented with cut glass pans and spangle drops, etc; do, do, gilt and bronze do; splendid Lustres ornamented with Paste drops, etc. of two, three and four lights. Grecian Lamps for halls and rooms, Entry Lamps in great variety, gilt, bronzed, two, three, or four branches.

In Figure 156 is given a very handsome pair of lamps. These may have been made at Sandwich, for at the time of their closing down they were at work on an order of lamps. These have cut-glass fonts and shades and moulded bases, and were of comparatively late make, as can be seen from the design of the brass fixtures.

*Figure 156, page 293.*

A blown glass lamp chimney is shown in Figure 157. These were used on metal lamps and were exceedingly fragile.

We are used to furnish our old bureaus and desks with clear or opalescent glass knobs when we wish to restore them to what we believe to be their original condition. Yet the following advertisement which appeared in the *American Daily Advertiser*, Philadelphia, for March 4, 1830, shows that there were many other colours for sale:

> Glass Commode Knobs. The Subscriber will furnish Glass Commode Knobs of the following descriptions, viz., Plain, Fluted, Fine Twisted, Coarse Twisted, Moulded and Sunflower, all of Superior Double Flint Glass. Also the same as the above of the following colours, viz. Deep Blue, Turquoise, Opal, Pearl, Agate.
>
> Orders will be received for the above of any size they may be wanted. They will be from the Jersey Glass Company, and in point of shape and quality of glass, not surpassed by any in the country; prices very low.
>
> Also, orders received for Cut Glass Knobs of any pattern required. On hand, an invoice of extra rich Cut Glass Knobs, and a few Signal Lanterns.
>
> M. NISBIT, 77 South Front Street, Philadelphia.

In addition to the glass knobs for furniture there were others much more ornate, really very beautiful, generally of opal glass, which were screwed into the wall to support mirrors, pictures, or to hold back curtains. In Figure 158 are shown three of these knobs, opal glass and decidedly alluring. Plain glass ones are shown in Figure 159 and one of them is turned to show the metal mounting.

*Figures 157-159, pages 294 and 295.*

The forger has been at work in reproducing these pretty things, but the character of the metal work betrays him. The late E. A. Barber sounded a warning about these curtain knobs as far back as September 24, 1911, in an article in the New York *Sun,* on "Old Glass and Its Imitations." He says:

"Pressed glass rosette curtain knobs in imitation of those produced at Sandwich, Massachusetts, about 1840 and later, are now being made in such large quantities that they have recently appeared in many of the principal 'antique shops,' and in auction sales in New York and Philadelphia. They are found in clear transparent glass and in white opalescent glass, and in colour and design closely resemble the old ones.

"These reproductions, however, are not dangerous, as they possess several features by which they may be recognized. The backs of the larger ones are well finished and present the appearance of sweating. The backs of the smaller ones are depressed to correspond with the relief design. The silvered or nickel-plated rods or shanks which run into them are fresh and bright and should deceive no one but the novice. Yet many of them are being sold to unsuspecting buyers, lovers of ancient things who do not take the trouble to examine them critically.

"The old examples are heavier and cruder in finish and are more or less nicked around the scalloped edges, while the metal rods are tarnished and possess the marks of age. The spurious examples which we have seen are three and four inches in diameter and possess six petals and scalloped edges. One lot recently sold by public auction was fitted with the usual metal rods or screws, which had been treated with acid or oxidized in spots to imitate the appearance of rust. As genuine pieces can be picked up at moderate prices, usually about $1.50 a pair, there would seem to be no good reason for purchasers being victimized by the sellers of cheap substitutes."

If reproductions were so abundant twelve or more years ago, there must be even fewer veritable antique ones to be found now. The ones shown are at the Metropolitan Museum of Art, New York.

Occasionally there are interesting bits of old glass, blown or moulded, which may be picked up in out-of-the-way places. True, the automobile has brought even the remotest hamlet within hailing distance of the dealer and collector, and there are many little old houses on back roads where clever imitations have been "planted" to deceive the enthusiastic but ignorant collector.

But old blown glass is almost unmistakable. A clear glass mug like the one in Figure 160, with its welted base and rim, crude handle and bubble-flecked bowl, speaks for itself. Why seek to assign it to some definite glass-works? To call it "Early American" seems quite identification enough.

*Figure 160, page 294.*

So with the next mug, Figure 161, a three-legged affair with not even the legs matching. No doubt this was one of the pieces made by a workman from the "corner pot" to please his own fancy. In the account of glass-making in this country, in the "Special Report of Manufactures," of the Tenth Census, there is this: "In 1837 there is a record of a 'vial works' and a 'black bottle factory,' the latter the only one of its kind in the Western Country." This factory made wine, porter and other black or amber bottles as well as demi-johns and carboys. The place where this was situated is not mentioned. This delightful three-legged mug may well have been made at a black-bottle factory.

The wine glass shown in Figure 162 is another pleasing piece. Probably this was made for home use, it seems far too irregular for a commercial piece. "Early American" can be used to describe this, and even so any one would welcome it to a place on their shelves.

Three very graceful wine glasses are shown in Figure 163. They are in the Buswell collection. They have the air-twist stems which are so desirable, and so infrequently found to-day. Although the glass in Figure 164 is called a medicine glass, it could be equally well used for a drinking glass. It is crude and rather heavy, but graceful in shape, and the term "Early American" covers this too. The rinsing bowl, Figure 165, is like many of its English cousins, two-eared and

*Figures 161-165, pages 296 and 297.*

moulded. There was not the abundance of wine glasses that there are now, when this was made, though there were many kinds of wine. So the glass was rinsed when changing from one kind of wine to another. The ribbed moulding used on this glass was used on a variety of glasses and glass vessels. Pitchers, bowls, decanters, bottles, bowls and tumblers all have it, and sometimes it extends to the pontil mark on the bottom, but not always. I own a decanter with the three rings on the neck, and the ribbing extends from the sides to the very crude pontil mark on the bottom. So crude is the workmanship that three or four ribs extend beyond the rest, and these are the only ones which show wear.

The last five glasses given are at the Metropolitan Museum, New York.

Cut-glass began to be advertised about 1830. In the Philadelphia directory for this year is this notice: "M'Cord and Shiner, manufacturers of Cut Glass, No. 3 & 7 Bank Alley, Back of the Merchants' Coffee House, Philadelphia. Setts of Glass Executed to order at the shortest notice. Workmanship warranted equal to any in the world, or no sale."

Thomas E. Walker and Co. (1830) at No. 15 North Fourth Street advertise: "Heavy English Tale and Flint Tumblers, rough and cut bottoms, ring and star bottom do; rough and star bottom Decanters, Pocket bottles, Flower Glasses, Lamp Shades."

There was competition not only by English but by

Irish glass-works too. Henry J. Pepper, 103 Chestnut Street, Philadelphia, was agent for Waterford glass. His name is given in the directory for 1830, and his name is mentioned in the Waterford account books.

Henry Chance, the great English glass-maker, in his paper, "On the Manufacture of Crown and Sheet Glass," sums up in a few words the difficulties of making perfect glass:

"Perhaps the glass has been badly melted and is seedy, that is, full of little vesicles, to which the rotary motion has given a circular shape; or the gatherer may have enclosed air within his metal and a gatherer's blister is the result—or a pipe blister, or pipe scales, or dust from the pipe-nose, or dust from the marver, or dust from the bottoming-hole, or dust from the nose-hole, or dust from the flashing furnace, or bad bullions, or scratches, or music lines may disfigure the table, or the glass may be crizzled, or curved, or bent, or hard, or smoky, or small, or light, defects to explain which would be a long and dreary task."

NEW YORK State was among the first states to engage in glass-making. In 1732 it is recorded that two factories were in operation. It was not till 1810, however, that American glass-works became of sufficient importance to attract attention, and that the Census returns include a statement of manufactured articles.*

There were many little glass-works scattered all about the state, and their product was small, and most of them were short-lived. The only records remaining are to be found in early gazeteers and county histories. Such accounts from these sources as I have been able to verify are found in the list at the back of the book.

In 1835 the Census reports thirteen glass-houses at work in New York State. The product of one of these, at Saratoga Springs, has not entirely disappeared, and Saratoga glass has been eagerly snapped up by such collectors as have been fortunate enough to secure it. In a New York State gazeteer (1860) mention is made of a glass-works being established at Mt. Pleasant, Saratoga County, in 1801.

Whether this date is too early I cannot say, but the glass which is now so eagerly sought by collectors dates

* Tenth Census.

considerably later.  My informant, Mr. S. M. Sterns of Saratoga Springs, says that the first Saratoga factory was started about 1835 on top of a mountain about twelve miles from Saratoga.  Wood was abundant, but all the materials for making glass were hauled up the mountain, made into glass and then hauled down.

Bottles only were made, some for spring water, others for pocket flasks of the same type as the "Success to the Rail Road" flasks.  While bottles were the regular product of the works, the glass-blowers were allowed to make for their own use all the dishes and small wares they desired, such as rolling-pins, canes, cans, bowls, balls, hats, darners, Jacob's Ladders, besides all kinds of table wares.  As the metal was furnished free of cost to the workmen, their homes were well supplied.

The glass objects were made in three colours, light green, a rich deep green, and olive.  A collection of this glass is shown in Figure 166.  The glass-blowers were evidently men of taste, as the shapes of the articles are very pretty, and their rich colouring makes them most attractive.

The workmen for this factory are said to have come from Rome, New York, and the factory was built and operated by the Granger Brothers.  Very recently there was still living one of the men who was a glass-blower at the Saratoga factory.

The second glass-works, erected at Saratoga Springs itself, was built by the Congress Spring Company.

*Figure 166, page 297.*

Mr. Sterns says: "The glass made by both of these companies is of great value. This section has been combed, raked and spaded, and the glass brings unheard-of prices. I think the hunt must soon end, as I spent two days last week with only one good vase as a reward of a cellar to garret search."

The workmen from the mountain factory came to the Congress Springs Company's works soon after they were opened, and the factory continued to operate till about 1900.

## BOTTLES AND FLASKS

BOTTLES and flasks, either for liquor or medicine, present an interesting field for many collectors. But while these bits of glassware may be of value historically, they can never make a collection as beautiful to look upon as table and domestic glass, owing to the similarity of shape and colour. Yet when we see the arrangement in Figure 168 we are almost tempted to retract this statement, for Mr. Buswell seems to have overcome these difficulties most successfully.

It is true that these bottles were originally made in many different colours—olive, light and dark blue, emerald and light green, claret, rich brown, amber, opalescent and clear glass. But the survivors seem to be chiefly olive and light green, clear glass and brown. They were made between 1808 and 1870 and were blown in engraved metal moulds.

One of these bottles, in log-cabin shape, marked "E. Z. Booz's Old Cabin Whiskey, 1840" on the roof, and "120 Walnut St. Philadelphia" on the end, is a favourite. They may be found in various shades of amber, pale green or clear glass. The Whitney Glass Works made these bottles in Philadelphia in the William Henry Harrison presidential campaign, and no

*Figure 167, page 298.*

[ 283 ]

doubt Booz did a good business selling them filled. In Figure 168 is one of these bottles and the mould it was made in. They belong to the Pennsylvania Museum of Fine Arts, Philadelphia.

The late Dr. Barber, in "American Glassware," divided these bottles into six classes, which is a sufficiently broad characterisation to cover even the large number which have come to light. A very admirable check list has been prepared by Stephen Van Rensselaer in a little book called "Early American Bottles and Flasks." It covers the subject exhaustively.

Dr. Barber's division is as follows:

*Type I.* Slender and arched in form, flattened and shallow; edges horizontally corrugated. Elongated neck, sheared mouth, scarred base.

*Type II.* Oval in form, flattened and shallow; edges ribbed vertically, sheared mouth, scarred base.

*Type III.* Almost circular in form, flattened and shallow; plain rounded edges. Shortened neck; sheared, collared, or beaded mouth; scarred or flat base.

*Type IV.* Calabash or decanter shape, almost spherical; edges corrugated, ribbed or fluted vertically. Long, slender neck, circular or many-sided; sloping collar or cap at top; smoothly hollowed or hollowed and scarred base.

*Type V.* Arched in form, flattened and deep; edges corrugated vertically. Very broad and short neck, narrow round beading at top; scarred or flat base.

*Type VI.* Arched in form, broad at shoulder and narrow at base; flattened and shallow (modern flask shape); plain and rounded edges. Medium neck, single or double beading at top. Smoothly hollowed or flat base. Occasionally sheared mouth and scarred base.

Early flasks are shown in Figure 169. They were made at the Albany Glass Works, which was opened

*Figures 168 and 169, page 299*

as early as 1786 and closed in 1815. One of these flasks is in light blue and one in amber. The figure is George Washington in uniform; reverse, a full-rigged ship.

An eagle flask, aquamarine, made at Kensington Glass Works, is shown in Figure 170. This flask conforms to Type II of Barber. It is at the Metropolitan Museum.

A flask made at Coventry, Connecticut, about 1825 is shown in Figure 171. The D in DeWitt Clinton is reversed, and the workmanship is more crude than is usual with flasks of this period. It is at the Toledo Museum. The colour is amber and the reverse shows a bust of Lafayette facing to the right.

The two flasks in Figure 172 were made at the Kensington Glass Works. One shows a bust of Franklin; reverse the same; no lettering. The colour is aquamarine, sheared mouth, scarred base. The other flask shows a bust of General Taylor and the legend, "Gen. Taylor never surrenders." Above this is the lettering "Dyottville Glass Works, Philadelphia." The later form of these flasks had collared mouths, and the lettering was omitted. These flasks are at the Metropolitan Museum.

When Kossuth, the Hungarian patriot, was in this country at least two flasks were struck off in his honour. One of them is shown in Figure 173. This flask belongs to the class listed as Type IV of Barber, and has on the side shown a side-wheel steamboat with the

*Figures 170-173, pages 300-302.*

words "U. S. Steam Frigate Mississippi, S. Huffsey." This flask was made about 1850.

Other Huffsey flasks are shown in Figure 174. The smaller flask shown in Figure 173 is the more unusual; it has a bust of Taylor with "Bridgetown, New Jersey," surrounding it; reverse, bust of Washington. This was made about 1855.

The three flasks representing the Baltimore Glass Works are shown in Figure 175. The two outer ones show Washington and Taylor in profile, facing right. Surrounding Taylor are the words "Baltimore Glass Works." These were made at the Federal Hill branch, which was established as early as 1790. The smaller flask shows Taylor in uniform, facing left, surrounded by the words "Baltimore Glass Works." These flasks, pint and quart size, were made in aquamarine and amber.

The five bottles shown in Figure 176 are of unusual interest, most of them coming from glass-works which only varied their window glass activities by making bottles. The first one, barrel shape, was a design much used by sellers of "Bitters," and is the most modern of the group. One in this shape and marked "Old Sachem Bitters and Wigwam Tonic" is not hard to find.

The flask marked "Liberty" is a product of the West Willington Glass Works, which operated in that place under different managements, from 1830 to 1872. The flask with the basket of flowers is one of two designs

*Figures 174-176, pages 302-304.*

made by the Lancaster Glass Works, at Lancaster, New York. It is a pretty bottle, in aquamarine, with sheared mouth and scarred base.

"Success to the Rail Road" was made at the Kensington Glass Works; reverse the same. It is a fine old bottle, amber, quart size. The stopper is one which you occasionally come across in a bottle which has been in a farmhouse home, and is a bit of a corn-cob. Whether it was put in because it was handy, or to improve the flavour, or to show that the contents was "corn likker," who shall say?

The fifth flask was made at the Westford Glass Works which opened 1857. It shows its comparatively modern origin by its double-ringed neck. These flasks are at the Metropolitan Museum.

A flask of considerable interest, maker unknown, is the deer and hunter one, shown in Figure 177. It is pint size, sapphire blue, and has an unusual base, which is scarred. The reverse shows a boar's head in centre, surrounded by oak leaves and acorns.

The other flask, with its spread eagle, was made at the Louisville Glass Works, which were opened in 1875 and operated by Capt. J. B. Ford. This flask is amber, but they also came in light green. The two flasks belong to the Pennsylvania Museum of Fine Arts.

The first flask in Figure 178 is another Lancaster, New York, one; it is pint size, aquamarine. The second one has a Masonic design, with twelve stones in the

Figures 177 and 178, pages 303 and 321.

[ 287 ]

pavement, and Masonic emblems around and outside the arch. The reverse has an eagle, facing left and perched on arrows, and an olive branch. Panel below contains the word "Keene." Amber.

The one with the clasped hands and the word "Union" may have been made by Huffsey, at the Whitney Glass Works, or at Pittsburg. The reverse is the same and the double-collared neck makes it later than the Kossuth and Jenny Lind bottles. Its colour is amber.

Gen. Taylor in uniform, facing left, with "Bridgeton, New Jersey," and a star encircling bust, is the fourth bottle. Washington is on the reverse, with the name above. Light green, pint size. These four bottles are the property of the Metropolitan Museum, New York.

Some pretty little flasks with pewter tops, similar to those made at the Louisville Glass Works, are shown in the next illustration, Figure 179. The designs are hearts and fleurs-de-lis. They belong to the Pennsylvania Museum of Fine Arts.

*Figure 179, page 322.*

Fig. 148. DOVE DESIGN

Fig. 147. BIRD PATTERN

(*See page* 250)

Fig. 149. BLUE AND CLEAR GLASS, STIEGEL

(*See page* 250)

Fig. 151.  MOULDED BOTTLE
Fig. 150.  EARLY BOTTLES

(See page 254)

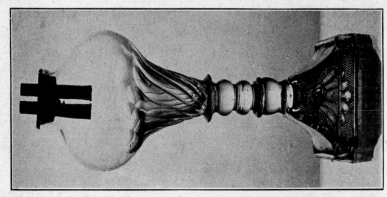

Fig. 154. GERMANTOWN LAMP

Fig. 153. EARLY LAMP

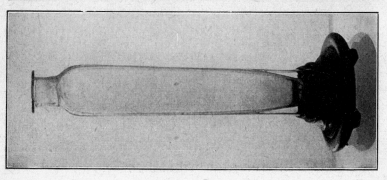

Fig. 152. EARLY PHIAL
(See page 25, col 256)

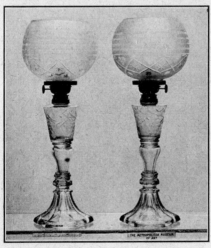

Fig. 155.  CLEAR GLASS LAMP
Fig. 156.  CUT AND MOULDED LAMP
(*See pages* 256 *and* 273)

[ 293 ]

Fig. 160.   CLEAR GLASS MUG

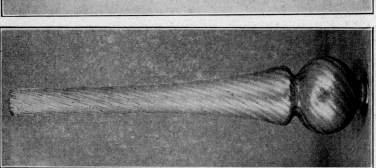

Fig. 157.   LAMP CHIMNEY

Fig. 158.  CURTAIN KNOBS, OPAL
Fig. 159.  CLEAR GLASS KNOBS

(*See page* 274)

Fig. 161. MUG WITH LEGS      Fig. 162. EARLY WINE
                                                          GLASS

Fig. 163. WINE GLASSES, AIR-TWIST STEMS

*(See page* 277)

Fig. 164.  MEDICINE        Fig. 165.  RINSING BOWL
        GLASS

Fig. 166.  SARATOGA GLASS

(*See pages* 277 *and* 281)

Fig. 167.   ARRANGEMENT OF BOTTLES AND FLASKS
(*See page* 283)

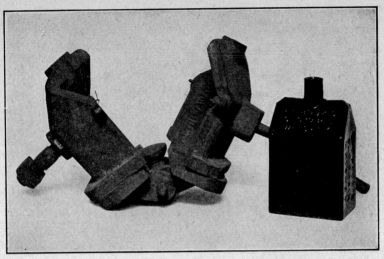

Fig. 168.  BOOZ BOTTLE AND MOULD
Fig. 169.  EARLY ALBANY FLASKS

(*See page* 284)

Fig. 171. COVENTRY, CONN, FLASK

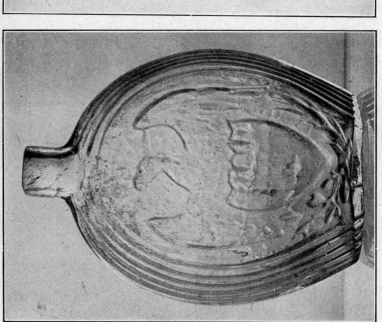

Fig. 170. KENSINGTON FLASK

(See page 285)

THE METROPOLITAN MUSEUM
OF ART.

Fig. 172. KENSINGTON FLASKS

(See page 285)

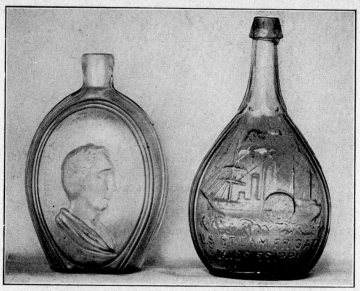

Fig. 173. KOSSUTH AND HUFFSEY BOTTLES
Fig. 174. HUFFSEY BOTTLES
(*See pages 285 and 286*)

Fig. 175.  BALTIMORE FLASKS
Fig. 177.  FLASKS

(*See pages 286 and 287*)

Fig. 176. BOTTLES AND FLASKS

(See page 286)

THE average collector who loves his glass for its own beauty, the pleasure he had in finding it, and the delight of possession, does not concern himself too deeply as to where it was made. For the owner of the three-section mould pieces this is a wise state of mind, for so far a large portion of this charming class of glass must come under the head of "Maker Unknown."

Almost all of the three-section mould pieces have a strong family resemblance, as to decoration at least, for the quilted and sunburst pattern is the one most frequently found. This glass is almost as agreeable to touch as to sight, and there are certain pieces which are most beguiling, even if the collector's fancy runs to glass in a particular colour, or to some one object, pitchers, salt-cellars, etc., or the product of some one glass-house.

There are small decanters, delightful little things with sunburst and quilted design and ball stoppers, holding perhaps a pint, which may be found occasionally. Recently I had one offered me as a piece of English glass, the dealer not being sufficiently well informed on this branch of American glass to recognise it.

The large decanters with the usual sunburst and quilted pattern are not so rare as the small ones. The decanter shown in Figure 180 is somewhat unique, since this one has the daisy-in-the-square pattern instead of the sunburst. This daisy pattern is spoken of later.

Many different pieces of table-ware were made in the three-section moulds, and saucers, bowls, one of the latter being nine and three-quarters inches in diameter, together with pitchers and a mug are shown in Figure 181. The bowls are very decorative with the quaint design on them, combined with ribbing and heavy welted edges.

One of the least common pieces is a sugar-bowl, in this three-section mould type of glass. A very fine one, in fact the choicest known, is shown in Figure 182. It is in the Buswell collection. The cover is most ornate and fits perfectly, which is not always the case.

It may be well to state here for the benefit of those who do not know this three-section mould glass, that instead of being blown into the ordinary moulds which had two sections, these moulds had three sections. The two-section mould glass showed two ridges where the moulds joined, and the three-section mould glass showed three. The moulds were never perfect enough not to show these ridges, and with use they grew larger, and always were in evidence.

Two pitchers, quilted and ribbed, are seen in Figure 183. Though attractive they are not so pretty as when

*Figures 180-183, pages 322-324.*

combined with the sunburst. Drinking glasses of many kinds were made in this type of glass, and a flip glass quilted and ribbed is given in Figure 184; a barrel-shaped tumbler, quilted and ribbed, is shown in Figure 185; and a wine glass with diagonal fluting in addition to the quilting and ribbing is shown in Figure 186.

The barrel-shaped tumbler and quilted salt-cellar given in Figure 187 are assigned to New Hanover, New Jersey, but I find no record of any glass-works established there. They are, however, exactly of the same type as the other three-section mould pieces, so I include them here. They, like the other three-section mould pieces with the exception of the sugar-bowl, are the property of the Metropolitan Museum of Art, New York.

*Figures 184-187, pages 325 and 326.*

THE glass made at Stoddard, New Hampshire, is also, some of it, blown in three-section moulds. In searching about for some glass-works where it is known that three-section mould glass was made, much incorrect information has been set afloat.

The kind of glass made at Stoddard was coarse in quality, and a dark amber-green in colour. Window glass, bottles and decanters were the chief output, and in the "History of Stoddard, N. H." by Isaiah Gould, published 1897, he says that the largest business carried on in the town was the manufacturing of glass bottles.

In Figure 188 are shown three Stoddard bottles or decanters, which belong to the Toledo Museum of Art. They show the quilted and sunburst design, are blown in three-section moulds, but are dark and heavy.

The first glass-works in Stoddard were built in 1842 by Joseph Foster, who came from Keene, New Hampshire, and "built a furnace, of stone principally, in an old house west from Gilson's Tavern, and ran it a short time, but having no capital he failed in business. He afterward built another 80 rods north of the village, but again failed."

"Gilman Scripture, John M. Whiton, jr., and Calvin

Figure 188, page 326.

Curtis built a large factory for making bottles at Mill Village in 1846, and were doing a profitable business. The next winter the factory was burned. It was soon rebuilt. They are (1854) making annually about $2500. worth of bottles of various sizes and descriptions."

The two bottles in Figure 189 show the crudeness of the metal. They belong to the Metropolitan Museum of Art.

While still continuing the dark amber-green colour of the glass, the two pitchers shown in Figure 190, three-section mould, are much better quality metal. The one with the wide quilted and sunburst band belongs to the Toledo Museum of Art, the other to the Metropolitan Museum.

The two glass inkstands in Figure 191 are also Stoddard and are at the Metropolitan Museum. They are coarse and dark but the decoration persists in the familiar pattern.

"Another factory was built in the south part of the town ( Stoddard) for the same purpose (making bottles) in 1850 by Luman Weeks, Almon Woods, Ebenezer A. Rice, Nicholas Hill and Fred A. Gilson, where they carried on business two years, when Messrs. Wood and Hill left the company; after another year Mr. Rice sold out; the business is (1854) carried on by Messrs. Weeks and Gilson; they are doing a good business but something less than the other company."

*Figures 189-191, pages 327-329.*

These notes were furnished me by Otis G. Hammond, Superintendent of the New Hampshire Historical Society, Concord, N. H. He also says that all the glass he has seen from these factories is coarse, dark, heavy metal.

Yet there has recently been ascribed to Stoddard, table-ware of a rich blue colour. There has also been sold at auction under the name of "Stoddard" a double-dipped pitcher, Wistarberg type and colour.

I am giving in Figure 192 two little clear glass hats. They are ascribed to Stoddard, but it is extremely doubtful if they were made there. Even though they show the quilted pattern, the alternating figure is not the sunburst, but the daisy-in-the-square, which was used sometimes by Stiegel. It is much more likely that they were made in South Jersey or Pennsylvania, both from the quality of the glass and the decoration. They are at the Metropolitan Museum.

Among the historical bottles there is one with an eagle design and the words "New Granite Glass Co." and on the reverse, "Stoddard, N. H." The firm which made this bottle must have been one of little importance, for Mr. Hammond of the New Hampshire Historical Society tells me that he finds no record of the incorporation of any such company, nor any mention of it.

There was not any large amount of money invested in glass-works in New Hampshire, at least during the

Figure 192, page 329.

first quarter of the nineteenth century. The "Special
Report of Manufactures of the Tenth Census" states
that in 1820 twenty-five thousand dollars was the sum
invested in glass-works in the state.

THE story of the glass-making business at Keene, New Hampshire, is clear enough, but the glass which was made there, chiefly bottles and decanters, seems to have almost entirely disappeared.

The following extracts from the "History of Keene," and from other records, have been furnished me by Mr. Hammond of the New Hampshire Historical Society.

The most important person connected with the glass industry of Keene was Henry Rowe Schoolcraft, L.L.D., U. S. Indian agent and author, who was born at Watervliet, N. Y., in 1793; was graduated at Union College in 1811; then learned the art of glass-making.

"His grandfather came from England, surveyed land, taught school, and changed the family name from Calcroft to Schoolcraft. His father, Laurence Schoolcraft, was superintendent of a glass factory near Albany, N. Y.—had been a soldier in the Revolutionary War, and a colonel in the War of 1812—came to Keene about 1814 as an expert to superintend the manufacture of glass, and remained several years.

"Henry came to Keene with his father, and the next year Daniel Watson, Timothy Twitchell and young Schoolcraft seceded from the company on Prison Street, united as partners, built a factory and made flint glass bottles and decanters on Marlboro Street, and had a store on Main Street, near the present Eagle Hotel. Afterward Watson, and still later Twitchell, withdrew. Nathaniel Sprague joined, and the firm became Schoolcraft and Sprague."

From the New Hampshire Laws, 1811-1820, it appears that the factory of Henry R. Schoolcraft and Nathaniel Sprague for the manufacture of glass in Keene, was exempted from taxation to the valuation of $10,000 by Act of June 26, 1816. The workmen, viz., one master stoker, two common stokers, two wood dryers, one calciner, one pot-maker, and five blowers were exempted from military duty. Act continued for five years, December 16, 1820.

The New Hampshire Glass Factory was exempt from taxation as well as Schoolcraft and Sprague. Their valuation was put at $15,000 and their workmen were exempt from military duty. The exemption from taxation was to continue five years.

In 1823 the Marlboro Street factory had passed into the hands of Justus Perry and John V. Wood. They continued the manufacture of glass bottles and decanters under the firm name of Perry and Wood. It was during their ownership that the bottles with eagle design and letters "P.W." were made.

By 1840 both glass factories were in operation, and for a short time a third one was in operation. By 1850 the Marlboro works were closed and the business moved to Stoddard. J. D. Colony and Co. were making window glass at the other factory, but late in this year this factory, a landmark for half a century, was destroyed by fire.

Like the Stoddard glass, that made at Keene was dark and coarse in texture. A letter from John J. Colony, of Keene, states that there was no very early manufacture of glass in Keene, and that window glass and bottles were the product of the works. He says that he remembers some of these bottles which were owned by his father, and they were decorated with crude designs, Masonic or patriotic, one or two of which were marked "Keene." But most of them had no designation whatever.

Among the historic bottles illustrated is one of these bottles marked Keene.

Apparently, however, the same rule was observed at Keene that was common at other glass-works, that the blowers were allowed to use the metal to make things for themselves. Mrs. Frederick Barrett, of Keene, owns two very handsome pitchers of a light green emerald glass, resembling Wistarberg in type, which were made at the Marlboro Street works at Keene, which at one time were operated by Mrs. Barrett's grandfather. The authenticity of these pitchers is undoubted.

## PITKIN GLASS

THE story of Pitkin glass can fortunately be written with a certainty which belongs to few other early American glass-works. The glass factory itself was in operation from 1783 to 1830, inclusive, at Manchester, Connecticut. The glass which was made there is well known though few authentic specimens exist, and those are so closely held that practically none come on the market.

The Pitkin family was prominent even before the Revolution. Captain Richard Pitkin and his sons William and Joseph were of such service to the Government during the trying days of the Revolution that they were granted the privilege of being the sole manufacturers of glass and snuff in the State of Connecticut for twenty-five years. That they made the glass is a matter of history; whether they ever made snuff is not known.

The factory was built in 1783, and the ruins of it are shown in Figure 193. The ruins are very picturesque and belong now to the Orford Parish Chapter of the Daughters of the American Revolution, who will keep them in as good preservation as possible. The grey stone walls are covered with vines, and a good-sized tree is growing out of the centre.

*Figure 193, page 330.*

The product of the factory was bottles and demi-johns, made from olive-green glass which is very bubbly. They occasionally made jars and inkstands. The factory was large enough to employ thirty men, and run on day and night shifts. There was not only a local but an export trade as well. After the bottles were blown they were taken in large quantities to Hartford by ox-team and shipped to the West Indies. The shipper was paid in rum and molasses.

In Figure 194 is shown a group of Pitkin glass. It belonged to the late Albert H. Pitkin, of Hartford, Connecticut, who was not connected with the Pitkins who were glass-blowers, but was an interested collector all the same. These pieces were shown at the Hudson-Fulton Celebration in New York in 1909. A great part of Mr. Pitkin's collection of pottery and glass was given to the Hartford Athenæum.

Like so much of this early American glass, the Pitkin glass, made for business purposes and not domestic use, was rough and crude. The bottles and demijohns, many of which were very large, had a great depression in the bottom, with a sharp bit of glass where the pontil was detached. The object at the end of the row in Figure 194 is a crude lump of the glass.

The factory continued in operation till 1830, when work was for some reason suspended and never resumed. Possibly it was lack of fuel, since wood was used, and no doubt the forty-seven years of operation

*Figure 194, page 330.*

had reduced the immediate supply, and made getting a sufficient quantity both difficult and costly.

The information about Pitkin glass was obtained from Mrs. J. M. Williams, of Manchester, Connecticut. Most of the Pitkin glass which is now owned in Manchester and vicinity came from the wagon factory belonging to Mrs. Williams' grandfather. He used many of the Pitkin bottles of all sizes to hold his paints, oils and varnishes. When his estate was finally settled up in 1900, the bottles were distributed among the townspeople.

Some of the demijohns are very large, with very squat bodies. These are seldom found. There is a pair owned in the Pitkin family which are used as fireside ornaments. Mrs. Williams herself owns a bottle with corrugated sides, which is very pretty, and more delicate than the others known.

Memorials of the works of the Pitkins, of which the factory is but one object, remain to this day. The epitaph on the tombstone of Esquire Richard Pitkin, who lies buried in the East Cemetery, reads:

"The shade-trees by the roadside will long perpetuate his memory, and to-day, more than eighty years since his death, the solid mile or more of elms and maples on Porter and Center streets are a living monument to his public spirit and a joy to the many passers-by."

# HISTORIC CUP PLATES

THE enthusiasm which so many collectors feel for the pressed glass cup plates have brought these little objects, which are not very pretty, prominently before the public. Originally they were made to sell for a few cents each, and it is by no means certain that all the different patterns which are so eagerly sought were made at Sandwich, Massachusetts.

In *Antiques* for February, 1922, is a list of patterns of these cup plates which is given here by permission.

SHIP CADMUS. Small design of ship under full sail in centre, enclosed in circle. Pattern on the edge varies in different specimens.

CHANCELLOR LIVINGSTON. There are three types of this design, showing a side-paddle steamboat. The name is impressed above and below the boat. See Figure 195.

THE BENJAMIN FRANKLIN. Also a side-paddle steamboat. The name Benjamin Franklin is printed above the boat. An imitation of this cup plate has recently been put on the market, and through the courtesy of *Antiques* we show them side by side. The genuine is nicked, and very clear, and in plain glass. The forgery is in blue glass, with perfect edge, the design shows up sharply. Figure 196.

PITTSBURGH STEAMBOAT. Marked "Union Glass Works, Pittsburgh, 1836."

THE FRIGATE CONSTITUTION. The design shows a frigate under full sail, on an octagonal cup plate. Very rare. In Figure 197 is given what is possibly a unique presentment of this design on a dish four and a half by seven inches. By permission of *Antiques*.

FULTON STEAMBOAT. Also on octagonal cup plate. Another rare piece.

THE MAID OF THE MIST. Made probably in the early 50's. A rare cup plate, but far less attractive than many other designs. It shows a picture of Suspension Bridge with the boat passing underneath it.

HENRY CLAY. There are six varieties of this favourite design. They show a bust of Henry Clay within a circle, surrounded by conventional

*Figures 195-197, pages 331-333.*

leaves. On most of the types the name "Henry Clay" surrounds the bust, but in one variety, the "N" is turned wrong-sided. The edge may be in single or double scallops. These Henry Clay cup plates are usually assigned to Sandwich, and most of them have that attractive edge, one large and two small scallops, which is thought to be from that factory. At the Toledo Museum of Art, in the Libby-Barber collection, is one of these cup plates in sapphire blue. One of the types is shown in Figure 198.

There is another cup plate marked "Henry Clay," with single scalloped edge, which is eagerly sought by collectors. The bust shows a head with curling hair, a ruffled cravat and upstanding coat collar. This is one of those misnamed pieces, like some of the Staffordshire busts. The border is stippled with floral designs at regular spaces, and it is a choice piece of glass.

GEORGE WASHINGTON. This is another choice piece and much sought after. The large head is placed upon a star in the centre and surrounded by a laurel wreath. Octagonal, with scalloped border.

RINGOLD-PALO ALTO. This plate was struck off to commemorate the death of Major Ringold at Palo Alto in 1846. This was at the opening of the Mexican War, and Major Ringold was a popular hero.

HARRISON. There are two types of this cup plate, one with the word "President" in a reserve space above the head, see Figure 198, and one showing the space without the lettering. Both of them show around the head the word "Major-Gen. W. H. Harrison, born Feb. 9, 1773." The Presidential one also has the date "1841."

LOG-CABIN, with cider barrel, flag and tree. This is to symbolise the Tippecanoe Hard Cider campaign. There are three patterns of this design, two with different borders of loosely grouped flowers, and a third with acorn border. One is shown in Figure 198.

FORT MEIGS LOG-CABIN. The log-cabin in the centre has above it the words "Fort Meigs." In the border is the word "Tippecanoe," and below the name "Wm. H. Harrison." See Figure 198.

LOG-CABIN, with flag. This is a small cup plate, showing in the centre a picture of a log-cabin with a flag on the ridge-pole, blowing in the breeze.

LOG-CABIN, with chimney. Less pleasing than the other log-cabin designs; the border is plain with wide-scalloped edge.

LOG-CABIN, with Liberty Cap on pole. A recent addition to the list.

BEEHIVE. Two types, both showing beehives in centre, the difference being in the border and quality of glass. Figure 195.

EAGLE, 1831. Figure of eagle in centre, facing left, and below it the date, 1831. Figure 198.

*Figure 198, page 334.*

EAGLE, with plain edge. This eagle faces right, there is no date and the edge is plain.

SMALL EAGLE, with dotted edge. Eagle faces right and about it are thirteen stars. Dotted edge.

GRAPE-VINE EAGLE. This is one of the rare patterns. Eagle in centre very small, with grape-vine border. The stippled work on border and scalloped and pointed edge are very pretty.

FLEUR-DE-LIS EAGLE. Eagle in centre very clear and fine, surrounded by a little rim of fleurs-de-lis alternating with small flowers. There is a stippled border with leaves and flowers.

EAGLE AND THIRTEEN STARS. A fine eagle in centre, grasping thunderbolts, and above it thirteen stars arranged in a semi-circle. Scalloped edge and floral border. Rare. See upper row, Figure 195.

EAGLE WITH THIRTEEN STARS IN SUNBURST. There are three varieties of this pattern, central design of eagle surrounded with a stipple ring set with thirteen stars, but with different borders and edges, one of them being plain. See Figure 195, lower row.

FORT PITT EAGLE. This design in two styles is highly considered, showing the eagle in the centre with scroll above, with the words "Fort Pitt," and twenty-four stars. This places the date of its issue between 1821 and 1836. Edge may be scalloped or plain.

HOP OR BLACKBERRY-VINE EAGLE. Small eagle surrounded by dots, and a vine border, edge plain.

BUNKER HILL. There are four variations in the Bunker Hill pattern. All have scalloped edges with a picture of the monument in the centre. The lettering on them varies, one form being, "Bunker Hill battle fought June 17, 1775." Another has in addition a second row of lettering which says, "From the Fair to the Brave." (See Figure 198.) Another one has an outside rim of printing which reads, "Corner stone laid by Lafayette, June 17, 1825. Finished by the Ladies." (Figure 198.) Collectors as a rule assign the Bunker Hill cup plates to Sandwich, but there are no records to back up this assumption. The general workmanship and quality of the glass is what they go upon, though Sandwich glass, so-called, varies from clear fine metal to that imperfectly cooked and full of bubbles and lines.

A cup plate has recently appeared with the design of a plow in the centre. It has a stipple border with leaves raying out from the centre medallion, and an edge of scallops and points.

There is a log-cabin tea plate made at the Whitney works (see Figure 199) probably about 1840, at the same time they made the log-cabin whiskey-bottle, which is the prettiest of any with this design. This piece is at the Toledo Museum of Fine Arts.

*Figure 199, page 335.*

Fig. 178. FLASKS AND BOTTLE

(*See page* 287)

Fig. 180. THREE-SECTION MOULD DECANTER

Fig. 179. FLASKS WITH PEWTER TOPS

(*See pages* 288 *and* 306)

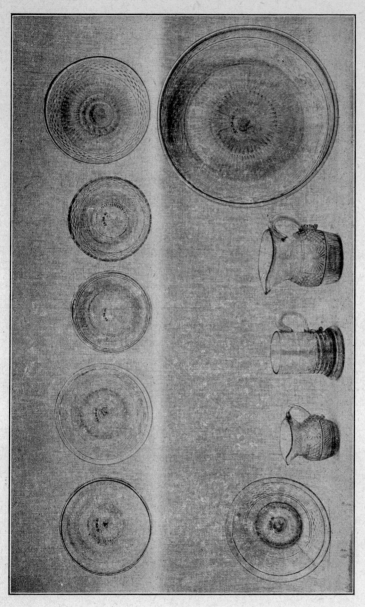

Fig. 181. GROUP OF THREE-SECTION MOULD GLASS

(See page 306)

Fig. 182. SUGAR BOWL, BUSWELL COLLECTION
Fig. 183. THREE-SECTION MOULD PITCHERS

(*See page* 306)

Fig. 184.  FLIP GLASS

Fig. 185.  BARREL-SHAPED GLASS      Fig. 186.  WINE GLASS

(See page 307)

[ 325 ]

Fig. 187. GLASS ASCRIBED TO NEW HANOVER, N. J.
Fig. 188. STODDARD, N. H., BOTTLES
(See pages 307 and 308)

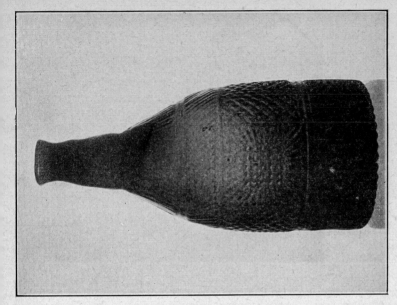

Fig. 189. STODDARD, N. H., BOTTLES

(See page 309)

Fig. 190.  TWO STODDARD PITCHERS

(*See page* 309)

Fig. 191. TWO STODDARD INKSTANDS
Fig. 192. TWO CLEAR GLASS HATS

(*See pages* 309 *and* 310)

Fig. 193.  RUINS OF PITKIN FACTORY

Fig. 194.  PITKIN GLASS

(*See pages 315 and 316*)

Fig. 195. GROUP OF CUP PLATES

(*See pages 318-320 and 337*)

Fig. 196.  BENJAMIN FRANKLIN CUP PLATES
Upper—Genuine, White.
Lower—Counterfeit, Blue.

(*See page* 318)

Fig. 197.  FRIGATE CONSTITUTION

(See page 318)

Fig. 198.  GROUP OF CUP PLATES

(*See pages* 319 *and* 320)

Fig. 199. LOG-CABIN TEA PLATE AND WHISKEY BOTTLE, WHITNEY WORKS

(*See page* 320)

Fig. 200. VIEW OF SANDWICH GLASS-WORKS, 1835

(See p. 338)

In addition to these historic cup plates there are many others which are extremely pretty, like the heart and dart design, some of which are assigned to Sandwich. Some are comic, like the one in Figure 195, with its lettering, "The wedding day and three weeks after."

It is possible, if all the patterns with their variations are found, to build up a collection of about forty historic designs alone. If you include others which rely on their decorative quality for their value, you are embarked on a search which practically has no end.

Unfortunately, like so many other things which are esteemed by the collector, these little glass trifles are being duplicated, and wary must be he or she who does not, unawares, allow some of these frauds to creep in among the veritable old ones.

*Figure 195, page 331.*

THE study of Sandwich glass and the gathering of collections of it are occupying many collectors at present. By the term "Sandwich," pressed glass is usually intended, though the Boston and Sandwich Glass Co. made both blown and cut-glass as well. A view of the works in 1835 is shown in Figure 200.

The name of Deming Jarves is closely bound up in the history of Sandwich glass, which is so much of a mystery. As to the correct dating of various patterns, whether or not they were made at Sandwich or the rival factory at New Bedford, Massachusetts, there is no information at hand.

There is a story about a carpenter inventing the first moulds used for pressed glass in this country, and that they were used at Sandwich, but like so many other tales about glass, it lacks confirmation. Deming Jarves says in his book on American Glass, that as early as 1815 he imported "pressed glass" from both England and Holland. He specifies salts, candlesticks, bowls, etc., and further states that from 1814 to 1838 "no improvement was made in this process." In passing it may not be amiss to say that some of those pressed glass articles from England and Holland were no doubt responsible

Figure 200, page 336.

for the dolphin which was used so freely in the Sandwich glass candlesticks, compotes, and other pieces. In Figure 201 are shown a group of these candlesticks, clear, canary, peacock and opalescent. They belong to Mrs. George W. Mitton, of Jamaica Plain, Massachusetts, whose fine collection of Sandwich glass is known to all who are interested in this beautiful product.

Dolphins were a favourite form of decoration with glass-makers as far back as the Middle Ages, among the Muranese workers at Venice, and were copied by glass-makers everywhere.

Deming Jarves was not only a glass manufacturer but an inventor as well, particularly of articles for glass-makers' use. On February 2, 1821, from Boston he took out a patent for a "machine for opening glass-blowers moulds." On December 1, 1828, from Boston, he obtained a patent for a method of "pressing melted glass into moulds." On June 13, 1829, and on October 19, 1830, he took out two patents for "Glass Knobs." On May 28, 1830, he took out one for a "glass-makers mould."

I have not been able to get descriptions of these patents from the Patent Office at Washington. The Patent Office Report, which is the earliest Patent Office publication, does not go back of 1846. They are not numbered, these early patents of Deming Jarves, and are buried deep in the Patent Office archives, if the subject matter is there at all.

*Figure 201, page 353.*

In October, 1846, he took out a patent for a glass furnace; this patent is numbered, 4783. It is interesting because it is for "a new and useful Improvement in Glass Furnaces, by which they may be operated by anthracite coal."

An article appeared in the Boston *Transcript,* September 4, 1920, by Charles Messer Stow, which gives to a certain extent the history of glass-making at Sandwich, Massachusetts, which covered a period from 1825 to 1888. This information is substantiated by a letter which I have received from Mr. George E. Burbank, a lifelong resident of Sandwich.

As to the beginnings of the industry, Mr. Stow states: "Early in 1825 a Boston man named Deming Jarves . . . called a meeting of the citizens of Sandwich, and told them that, if there was sufficient interest manifest in Sandwich, he would build a glass-works there."

Mr. Jarves himself writes of the start: "Ground was broke in April, 1825, dwellings for the workmen built and manufactory completed; and on the Fourth of July, three months from the first breaking of ground commenced blowing glass."

The start was modest, only an eight-pot furnace holding 800 pounds each, 7,000 pounds weekly.

Mr. Stow continues: "The location at Sandwich was not on account of the sand, but that there was a large amount of timber available near by, and the works used wood for fuel. The policy of Mr. Jarves was to buy land with timber on it, and the agent who was in charge of the works, besides having authority to buy land, had also the duty of seeing to the erection of the workmen's houses. It seems that he exceeded his authority somewhat, and soon Mr. Jarves found that he needed more capital than he possessed to carry out the ambitious plans which had been developed. Therefore he formed a stock company, and the 'Boston and Sandwich Glass Company,' was incorporated on February 22, 1826, by Deming Jarves, Henry Rice, Andrew T. Hall and Edward Monroe. At this time from 60 to 70 men were employed and the manufactured goods amounted to about $75,000 worth. The glassworks prospered from the start and regularly and gradually expanded, employing more and more men, and turning out more and more glass."

In a paper by A. F. Dorflinger called "Development of the Cut Glass Business in the United States," 1902, he says that the Boston and Sandwich Glass Company used 3,000 cords of wood yearly. When they increased the size of the furnace to four furnaces of ten pots each, the amount of wood consumed was much greater. No wonder Mr. Jarves busied himself in inventing and perfecting a furnace for glass that would burn coal: "the importance of a furnace in which this kind of fuel can be used to advantage, will be apparent to every glass manufacturer," says Jarves himself.

"By 1854 the capitalization had reached $400,000

and five hundred men and boys were employed, and the value of the goods manufactured each year was $600,-000." The company looked out well for its workmen. Houses were built which were sold on the installment plan, but which the workmen were allowed to occupy at once. Stores were opened. More and more land was bought, and Sandwich town prospered on account of the glass-works.

"From 1825 to 1858 the finished product was transported to Boston entirely by water and the company owned the sloop 'Polly' which was able to come up a small creek almost to the door of the factory. In 1858 what is said to have been the first railroad of its kind in the United States was built to carry the barrels of finished product from the factory to the wharf, farther away from the landing on the creek, for that was to be negotiated only at high tide, and the growing business of the company demanded more frequent transportation than the tide afforded. In later years the company bought the steamer 'Acorn' and used it to compete with the Old Colony Railroad and drive down freight rates." *

It is generally assumed that the pressed glass found in Boston and vicinity is Sandwich, and that found in Pennsylvania was made in that state. But an immense amount must have been distributed all over the country by means of the annual auction sales. It is interesting

*Stow.

to note that Jarves himself did not claim for the Boston and Sandwich Glass Company superiority in the pressed glass line. He says in his book, published 1865, that "James B. Lyon and Co. of Pittsburgh are conceded to have made the choicest pressed glass, which was of such a superior quality that it was difficult to tell it from cut."

The Boston and Sandwich Glass Company was not the only one in which Deming Jarves was interested. In 1837 he started the Mt. Washington Glass Company in South Boston for his son George D. Jarves. A large shop for glass-cutting was run in connection with the glass-works. By 1840 they were making cut-glass bowls, salts, dishes, sugars and creamers, tumblers, stemware, decanters, lamps and globes. In 1850 the business was transferred to Jarves and Commerais. They started off with great éclat, but the business only lasted about ten years. A man named Patrick Slane tried to revive the works, but they were finally burned down.*

Getting his son started did not absorb all of Jarves' time. In 1850 a glass bowl was made and presented to Daniel Webster by the Boston and Sandwich Glass Company. In an accompanying letter by Mr. Jarves, he says regarding the bowl: "It claims the merit of being much the largest piece of flint glass made by machinery in any part of the world. Two machinists

* Dorflinger.

were employed six months in forming the mould. This bowl is the first made in this mould, and it is called 'the Union Bowl.' The name will not render it any less valuable." * There are no traces anywhere of this bowl or any made in this mould.

Deming Jarves remained with the Boston and Sandwich Glass Company till 1858. Then, after a quarrel with the directors, he withdrew, formed the Cape Cod Glass Works, to run in competition with the Boston and Sandwich Company. But this company was never very strong, and it only continued a short time after the death of Jarves in 1869.

The Boston and Sandwich Glass Company made a fine quality of flint glass. They used much good lead and the result was a clear ring to the glass when struck. Figures 202 and 203 show examples of their clear and frosted glass; they belong to the collection of Mrs. G. W. Mitton, of Jamaica Plain, Massachusetts.

"During its long career from 1825 to 1888 the works at Sandwich turned out glass of all sorts for all sorts of uses. In the early days came the pressed articles which are now in demand. Also some of the curious millefiori paper-weights. Later it made full sets for the table, goblets, tumblers and all kinds of wine glasses, with finger bowls and other accessories. These were plain, cut, etched, or engraved. About 1860 the management sent a man to Europe to study the process of

* History of Cape Cod.
*Figures 202 and 203, pages 354 and 355.*

acid etching and he brought back a machine which was
used to the company's profit both for table-ware and
commercial purposes. At one time the company were
turning out glass shades in between forty and fifty patterns, and many of these were etched." *

To the collector the most desirable product from
Sandwich is the coloured glass. Mr. Stow says that
some of the opal glass lamp-shades were from six to
sixteen inches across and very difficult to blow. Besides the opal there was much ruby glass turned out,
and it was coloured by the use of gold, which gives it
a brownish cast in some lights. They made some shades
in ruby, too, and many perfume bottles. A pair of
these is shown in Figure 204. They are at the Metropolitan Museum. In Figure 205 are shown two decanters, honey-coloured and amethyst. They belong to
the Toledo Museum.

"The stockholders of the B. & S. Glass Co. have
reduced the capital stock from $400,000 to $200,000.
It is stated that the introduction of the company's goods
into the West Indies promises to build up a considerable business for them." †

The company's export business became very large.
In later years the lamps they turned out went all over
the world. They made cruets for various uses and
tumblers, "at one time 500 tumblers every five-hour

* Stow.    † *American Pottery & Glassware Reporter*, 1879.
*Figures 204 and 205, page 356.*

shift, and bottles and jars of all sizes." Figures 206 and 207.

By 1880 the little town of Sandwich saw nothing but prosperity ahead. The Boston and Sandwich Glass Company were employing about 300 men and boys, at wages varying from four to six dollars a day. "Most of the men owned their homes, there was plenty of work, and they had confidence that the 'Flint Glass Workers Union' to which they belonged would assure them a continued prosperity for an indefinite time." But for mutual protection and trade advantages the Sandwich Company and other glass manufacturers formed the Flint Glass Manufacturers' Association.

At the end of December, 1887, the Association drew up an agreement which was presented to the workmen at the various factories. The men of Sandwich refused to accept it, and the glass company, which had been running at a loss for some time, issued an ultimatum. If the fires were allowed to go out they would never be relighted. But the men did not believe this. So the fires went out, the plant was closed and has never been reopened.

The buildings stood till 1920, when they were torn down to make place for a factory where wood pulp and soap were to be made. The old building where Deming Jarves started the Cape Cod Works has been altered into a plant for cutting veneer.

The closing of the works brought great hardship to

*Figures 206 and 207, pages 356 and 357.*

the glass-blowers and their families. Many of them owned their own houses and had grown up in the business. There was no demand for so many houses, and many lost the savings of years, and no doubt when too late regretted listening to the trouble-makers.

Ten of the men did not leave Sandwich to look for work elsewhere. They formed the Sandwich Co-operative Glass Company in 1888, put up a building and went to work. The venture was a failure.

There are few of the Sandwich pieces which can have definite dates of manufacture assigned to them. As far as any one knows, the little boat-shaped salt, marked "B & S Glass Co." and "Sandwich" on the bottom is the earliest. There is much discussion as to why it is lettered "Lafayet," but it seems to be a matter of lack of space for more letters, and it sounded all right when pronounced.

Through the kindness of *Antiques,* three views of this little salt are given, in Figure 208. It is much to be regretted that the works dropped the admirable idea of marking their product; collectors who call their treasures "Sandwich" just because it is pressed would never have got in the running.

It is customary to say that the Boston and Sandwich Glass Company made pressed glass from 1825 to 1888. But from 1860 to the close of the works they made blown table-ware in great variety, cut-glass of more

*Figure 208, page 358.*

or less excellence, Figure 209, and great numbers of lamp-shades.

"Boston and Sandwich Glass Co. (factory at Sandwich, Mass.) are running one eleven pot furnace. The manufacture consists principally of blown and pressed tableware, bar and fancy goods, together with a large line of decorated shades, crystal chandeliers, gas globes, etc. In ordinary pressed ware they have been unable to compete with Western factories, and are giving particular attention to the production of cut, etched, silvered and decorated wares." *

Although I have placed Sandwich glass last in these brief sketches of early American glass, it should by rights be among the leaders. But hope springs eternal, and all the years I have spent trying to learn about glass have been cheered by the idea that somehow, somewhere, I should find authentic data of what goods were made at Sandwich in pressed glass. But I have not been successful. Hundreds of letters, following up clues of every description, advertising for information, searching newspapers and getting others to search also, in hopes of finding an advertisement putting forth lists of goods made by the Boston and Sandwich Glass Company have brought nothing definite.

So I am giving as illustrations pieces from such well-known collections as that of Mrs. George W. Mitton, of Jamaica Plain, Massachusetts, who has studied and

* *American Pottery & Glassware Reporter*, 1879.
*Figure 209, page 359.*

handled hundreds of pieces of this glass; from the Metropolitan Museum of Art, New York; from the Toledo Museum of Fine Arts; and from *Antiques,* published in Boston. In Figures 210 and 211 are given some specimens of opaque white, clear and clear and coloured glass. The little compote in 210 is at the Metropolitan Museum, and the pieces in 211 at the Toledo Museum.

The Sandwich salts alone would form a collection of great beauty, for they range in colour from clear glass to a rich dark green, deep blue, and many shades from honey to amber. Few collectors have secured as many and as perfect pieces as Mrs. Mitton, and she owns numbers of specimens of that splendid shade of purple which was made at Sandwich, generally in objects of worth and fine design. All the pieces shown in Figure 207 are in this royal purple and canary yellow, which, by the way, no real collector would ever call vaseline, a dealer's term. In Figure 212 the compote in the upper row is ruby, the swan's yellow and opalescent, the candlestick deep amber, and the celery holder deep purple.

Of course the pitcher in the lower row is the most unusual of all, and is deep green flecked with gold, and the dolphins at the base are opal. Mrs. Mitton classes this as Sandwich because there are other gold flecked pieces which are supposed to have been made there.

Figure 213 shows some of the lamps which were

*Figures 210-213, pages 360-362.*

made in such numbers at Sandwich. All of them in this picture are coloured, medium sapphire, purple and canary yellow. The candlestick in the centre is purple, and the two on either side are dark blue. The covered dish is canary and the two openwork dishes are one blue and one green.

Deming Jarves, writing in 1854 concerning the condition of the glass industry in the United States, says: "In enumerating all the concerns, companies and corporations that have been engaged in the manufacture of flint glass in the Atlantic States, we find that the number is forty-two, of which number two concerns have retired and ten are now in operation: viz., two at East Cambridge, three at South Boston, one at Sandwich, three near New York City, and one at Philadelphia. This leaves two concerns who retired with property, and twenty-eight out of forty-two concerns, entire failures, the fate of the remaining ten to be determined by future events."

The business both local and export was so large there seems to have been little advertising done. A store in Boston was maintained from 1830 to 1888 at different addresses in Milk, Federal and Franklin streets. From 1874 to 1884 they had stores at 164 Devonshire and 21 Federal streets, but persistent search of the files of newspapers of the day have yielded nothing, so far.

Here I leave these fragments, in hopes that the next searcher may go farther and fare better.

## MEXICAN GLASS

MANY people are familiar with the decorative arts of Mexico—pottery, jewelry, rug-making and baskets. Less well-known, however, is the glassware, which is not only beautifully incised or carved, but further enriched with painting, chiefly in gold.

It appears that the making of glass began in Mexico soon after the conquest. It became an important industry, and continued so for two hundred years.

In a Bulletin of the Pennsylvania Museum for 1908, the late Dr. E. A. Barber declares that in his opinion this style of glass was made at Puebla, Mexico. A group of this glass belonging to the Pennsylvania Museum of Fine Arts, Figure 214, speaks for itself as to its beauty.

To support Dr. Barber's contention as to the source of this glass he quotes from "A New Survey of the Indies," written by Thomas Gage in 1648. This writer states that there was a glass-house at Puebla at that date, and that it was a rarity, none other being known,

Another writer, Betancurt, 1698, says that the glassware of Puebla surpassed that of all New Spain. Frey Juan Villa Sanchez, writing in 1745, declares that the glassware made in Puebla was not duplicated anywhere else in the kingdom, and equals that of Venice.

*Figure 214, page 363.*

Some very pleasing specimens are shown in Figures 215, 216, 217. They belong to the Metropolitan Museum of Art. Besides these examples at the Pennsylvania Museum and at the Metropolitan there are some pieces at the Smithsonian Museum at Washington, D. C. They are of similar incised and gilt decoration, and consist of a pitcher and covered dish.

The card attached reads, "Presented to Major-General E. O'C. Ord, U. S. Army, in 1881, by Manuel Gonzales, President of Mexico." They are loaned to the Smithsonian Museum by Captain J. T. Ord, U. S. Volunteers.

Glass is still made in Mexico, at Puebla, but the wares are simple flasks, bottles and drinking vessels. They are generally clear in colour, and of pleasing shapes, but there is none made now in cut and gilded style.

Some of the modern glass is shown in Figure 218.

Many inquiries as to the best way to clean old glass have been sent to me. The following has been recommended, though some strong soap diluted with water, shaken well in the glass object with a handful of shot, has always answered the purpose for me.

"To clean glassware: Break a few raw egg-shells into the article to be cleaned, with a little cold water, warm water if the article is greasy, shake well and rinse with fresh water. The glass will shine."

*Figures 215-218, pages 363-364.*

Fig. 201. SANDWICH GLASS DOLPHINS

(*See page* 339)

Fig. 202. CLEAR SANDWICH GLASS

(*See page* 344)

Fig. 203.   CLEAR AND FROSTED SANDWICH GLASS
(*See page* 344)

Fig. 204. RUBY SANDWICH GLASS     Fig. 206. SANDWICH
                                                        GOBLET

Fig. 205. AMETHYST AND HONEY-COLOURED DECANTERS

(*See pages* 345 *and* 346)

[ 356 ]

Fig. 207. SANDWICH JUG AND CELERY GLASSES

(*See page* 346)

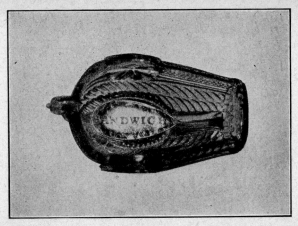

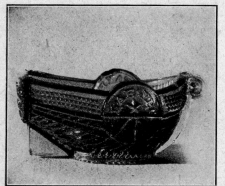

Fig. 208. B. & S. BOAT-SHAPED SALT-CELLAR

(See page 347)

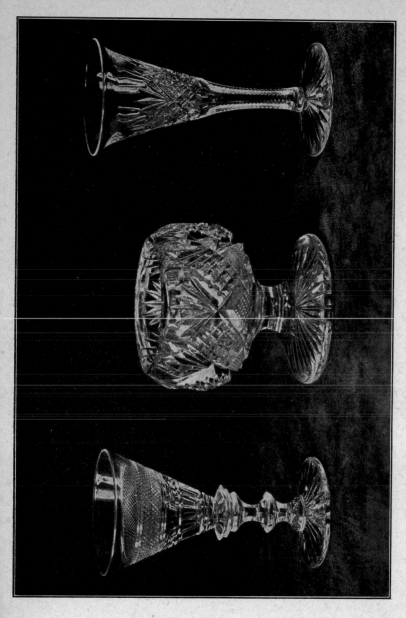

Fig. 209. GLASS, SANDWICH

(See page 348)

Fig. 210. OPAQUE SANDWICH GLASS

Fig. 211. OPAQUE AND CLEAR SANDWICH GLASS

(*See page* 349)

Fig. 212.   COLOURED SANDWICH GLASS

(*See page* 349)

Fig. 213.   SANDWICH GLASS

(*See page* 349)

Fig. 215.  MEXICAN PITCHER
Fig. 214.  GROUP OF MEXICAN GLASS
*(See pages* 351 *and* 352)

Fig. 216. MEXICAN      Fig. 217. MEXICAN VASE
COVERED VASE

Fig. 218. MODERN MEXICAN GLASS

(*See page* 352)

*View of the Glass Works of* T.W.DYOTT *at Kensington on the Delaware n° Philad°*

Fig. 219

(*See page* 373)

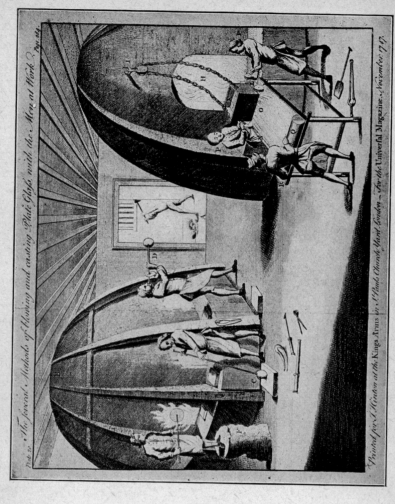

Fig. 220. INTERIOR OF OLD GLASS WORKS

(See page 374)

Fig. 222. EARLY DECANTERS

(*See page* 379)

Fig. 221. GLASS FROM KENSINGTON GLASS WORKS
Fig. 223. CUT-GLASS BY CRAIG RITCHIE
(*See pages* 376 *and* 382)

## AMERICAN GLASS FACTORIES

THIS list has been gathered from newspapers, town records, histories, gazeteers, county publications, anywhere in fact that they could be found. In some cases where the records overlap the dates vary a little, but I have left them as I have found them. My intention was not to list anything later than 1850, but in some cases where operation has continued I have set it down. The list is far from complete, but it is at least a step towards gathering the records of this early and interesting industry.

ADAMS GLASS CO. Incorporated, 1812, in the town of Adams, Mass.

ALBANY, N. Y. Van Rensselaer Glass Works, said to have been opened as early as 1807.

ALBANY GLASS WORKS. See *Guilderland*.

ALEXANDRIA, VA. Glass works established, 1787. M. De Warville visited these works in 1788 and declares five hundred hands were employed.

ALLOWAYSTOWN, N. J. See account of Caspar Wistar.

AMELUNG, A. F. Frederickstown, Md. Glass factory established in 1797. Some of his German workmen started to cross the mountains to build a glass-works at what is now Louisville, Ky., but were stopped and taken to New Geneva, Pa., by Albert Gallatin. Amelung is said to have presented to General Washington two flint glass goblets made at his works.

BAKEWELL AND PAGE. Some Germans started a glass factory in Frederickstown, Md., which was soon abandoned. They went to Pittsburgh and started again, but were unsuccessful here. In 1808 this plant was taken up and run by Bakewell and Page, with one furnace of six twenty-inch pots, followed in 1814 by a ten-pot furnace. In Cramer's *Navigator* for 1813, it states in connection with Bakewell and Page that they have lately built another flint glass house, making two that they have in operation, and that "glass-cutting is likewise executed in this place, not inferior to the best cut-glass in Europe." A German named Eichbaum is said to have started a cutting-shop in Pittsburgh in 1809, and obtained his glass from Bakewell and Page.

The firm name was Bakewell and Anderson, 1820. Bakewell and Co., 1824. The works were burned down in 1845, but were rebuilt, and were operated under the name of Bakewell, Pears and Co., till about 1880. In 1879 they advertise in the *Pottery and Glassware Reporter* that they are: "Manufacturers of Crystal and Opal glass Table-ware, Bar Furniture, Druggists' Furniture in Crystal and Flint. Gas, Kerosene, Opal, Cone Shades, Globes, Smoke-bells, Round Ornamental Shades and Flint Glass Chimneys. Lantern Glasses and all Kinds of Blown and Pressed Ware made to order."

BALTIMORE GLASS WORKS. 1790. Established on a branch of the Patapsco River, at a place known as Spring Gardens. Another branch was started at about the same time at Federal Hill, Hughes Street. They made both amber and aquamarine bottles, which were marked "Baltimore," and "Glassworks." Washington design. The present works date from 1853, and they started to make flint glass in 1873.

BELTZHOOVER AND WENDT CO. 1813. Birmingham, Pa.

BOSTON CROWN GLASS CO. In July, 1787, Messrs. Whalley, Hunnewell and Co. received a charter allowing them the exclusive right to make glass in Massachusetts for fifteen years, and a fine of £500 was attached to any infringement of this right. Work was not really begun till 1792 owing to the difficulty in obtaining workmen, etc. In 1811 works in Essex Street were erected, but the War of 1812 prevented the successful operation of the works, but they were operated later, only to fail in 1826.

BRIDGETON, N. J. Glass-works established by Stratton, Buck and Co., 1837, and run till 1841. Operated under the name of Joel Bodine and Sons, 1848-1855. At latter date works were purchased by Potter and Bodine, and then a stock company was formed called the "Cohansey Glass Manufacturing Co." Made flasks in aquamarine with Washington design, marked "Bridgeton, New Jersey."

BROOKLYN. Loderwick Bamper. 1754.

BROWN'S PINES, N. J. 1800.

BROWNSVILLE, PA. According to the memorial sent to Congress in 1831 there were "four or five glass-works" at Brownsville.

CHELMSFORD, MASS. Window glass was made as early as 1802 in Chelmsfordtown at Middlesex village, by Hunnewell and Gore of Boston. This town is now a part of Lowell. In 1820, according to Allen's "History of Chelmsford," the works were in a flourishing condition, but they failed in 1826-27 and about this time were burned down. In 1828 the works were rebuilt, but were apparently unprofitable, since in 1839 the works were abandoned, and the company moved to Suncook village, Pembroke, N. H. On July 4, 1839, the Chelmsford Glass Co., Pembroke, N. H., was incorporated to make glassware, window glass, and glass plates. All trace and record of this glass-works has disappeared, except that there is still a street in the town called Glass Street. The New Hampshire Historical Society, at Concord, N. H., owns two or three specimens of this glass which came from residents of the town of Pembroke. They are described as of a "beautiful light green colour and fine texture."

CHESHIRE CROWN GLASS WORKS. Cheshire, Mass. In 1812 a factory was started here to make window glass. In 1852 the product was changed to plate glass. They operated only about two months, and then moved to Brooklyn, N. Y.

CHESTER GLASS COMPANY. Chester, Mass. The factory was started here in 1812, was incorporated in 1814. This company as well as the preceding one used the local sand, which was of excellent quality.

CLARK'S GLASS WORKS Washington, D. C. 1837.

COLUMBIA, N. J. 1812-1833. Window glass only.

CORNING GLASS WORKS. Corning, N. Y. In 1852 Amory Houghton, Sr., built and operated the Union Glass Works at Somerville, Mass., and ran them till 1864. He then sold out and bought the South Ferry Glass Works in Brooklyn, N. Y. He ran these till 1868, when he moved them to Corning, N. Y. In 1875 the business was reorganized under the name of the "Corning Glass Works," and is still in operation. They make exquisite glass of all kinds, particularly in colours.

COVENTRY, CONN. The Coventry Glass Works were organised by some citizens of that place as a stock company, in 1813. They made hollow ware, decanters and tumblers, and later, flasks with designs on them, snuff jars and inkstands. In 1820 the business passed into other hands, and from 1820 to 1830 it was operated by Thomas Stebbins and his successors, Stebbins and Chamberlin. In 1830 Gilbert Turner and Co. purchased the plant and worked it till 1848, when the supply of fuel, wood, gave out, and the works were closed. They made some of the earliest historic flasks, Lafayette and DeWitt Clinton, to commemorate the opening of the Erie Canal, 1825. These flasks are marked "S. & C." and "Coventry C-T."

CRAIG AND O'HARA. Pittsburgh, Pa. They opened glass-works in 1797. The site has been occupied continuously by glass-works. In 1880 they were called the Point Bridge Works, of Thomas Wightman and Co. It was one of the first works to use coal. Up to 1810 no glass-houses except those in Pittsburgh used coal.

Crystal Glass Co., Pittsburgh, Pa., made much household glass with a beehive. Sometimes below it was the motto, "Be industrious." Also bread-trays with a sheaf of wheat, oval; and they were constantly adding to their list of patterns. They made in 1880 "butter plates" with portraits of James A. Garfield and Winfield S. Hancock.

CUNNINGHAM AND CO., Pittsburgh. There is a bottle with the design of an Indian, marked with this name.

CURLING AND PRICE. Pittsburgh. They operated in 1828 what was known as Fort Pitt Glass Works. They were succeeded by E. D. Dithridge and Co., who were bought out by F. Lorenz, and he was succeeded by Thomas Wightman & Co.

"The Rev. Dr. Berley wrote to the St. Louis *Democrat*, 1879, that he baptised Henry Clay in his parlour at Ashland, at the same time administering this ordinance to his daughter-in-law, Mrs. Thomas Clay, on the 22nd of June, 1847, a few special friends being present. The water was applied by the hand out of a large cut-glass urn, which, among his many presents, had been given him by a manufacturer in Pittsburgh, Pa. It is said this urn was the largest piece of cut-glass then known. Mr. Clay was then seventy years old. He was subsequently publicly confirmed in the church. This piece of glass was made at the old Fort Pitt factory on Washington Street, then operated by Curling, Robinson & Co., in 1844, by Edward Dithridge, and presented by Mr. Curling to Henry Clay. It was the largest piece of cut-glassware which had been made at the time, and few have excelled it in either size or appearance. These facts we get from Mr. E. D. Dithridge, of the Dithridge Chimney Co., Ltd., son of the man who made the urn."—*American Pottery and Glassware Reporter*.

Kate Field's "Romance of Glass Making" shows the glass bowl used by Henry Clay in 1840. It was exhibited at the Chicago World's Fair, 1893, side by side with a piece of modern cut-glass, one of those over-cut pieces of heavy glass which were so popular at the moment. The picture of these two pieces is in Miss Field's little book, and a mere look establishes the superiority of the former.

Washington Beck during the 70's made many moulds of dishes and other pressed glass objects in "crystallo style" for the Fort Pitt works.

DENNY AND BEELEN. Pittsburgh. 1800. They built a glass-works on the north side of the Ohio, in that part of Allegheny known as Manchester.

DORFLEIN, PHILIP. Philadelphia. Was a mould-maker for bottles and other glassware from 1842 to 1900.

DORFLINGER, CHRISTOPHER. 1852. In this year Mr. Dorflinger organized a firm in Brooklyn. Early in the 60's he built the Greenpoint Works, and Hoare and Daily worked a cutting-shop in connection. In 1867 the White Mills Works were built which are still in operation.

DUMMER, GEORGE AND P. C. In 1824 they began to build a flint glass works in Jersey City. These works continued making glass for forty years, but were discontinued about 1860.

DUNBARTON, N. Y. Oneida County. Had a glass-works about 1802.

DURHAMVILLE, N. Y. Oneida County. Also had a glass-works about the same time.

DYOTTVILLE GLASS WORKS. Kensington, Pa., 1771. (See Figure 219.) They were founded by Robert Towars, leather dresser, and Joseph Leacock, watchmaker, on Bank Street. The next year the premises were sold to John and Samuel Elliot, who took Isaac Gray into partnership. They built additional furnaces and made bottles chiefly. In 1780 the property was sold to Thomas Leiper, tobacconist, who made bottles for his snuff. He kept the place twenty years. In 1800 the owners were Joseph Roberts, Jr., James Butland and James Rowland. They did business under the name of Butland and Co. In 1804 Rowland became owner and under the firm name of James Rowland and Co. they were operated till 1833. In this year they were bought by Dr. Thomas W. Dyott, who in 1838 was convicted of fraudulent insolvency, and the works were idle for some years. In 1843 they were leased by Henry Benners and under different owners have been in operation ever since.

Among the things made by Dr. Dyott when he was operating the Kensington works were three patterns of bottles, and on each of them he placed a portrait bust of himself in connection with some American patriot. Two of these bottles or flasks show the portrait of Benjamin Franklin, and on the reverse, T. W. Dyott; and on the third is a portrait of Washington, reverse, American eagle with shield, arrows, etc., perched on an oval which contains the initials "T. W. D." Around the edge is the inscription, "Kensington Glass Works, Philadelphia." On the other side is "Adams and Jefferson, July 4, A. D., 1776." As late as 1831 the furnaces were crude affairs, designed to run only six months in the year. At this time the Dyottville factory was the most extensive in the United States, melting about 800 lbs. of batch a day and producing vials, bottles, shop furniture, etc. In 1833 this works had five furnaces and from 250 to 300 men and boys were constantly employed. A contemporary picture of the works is shown in Figure 219.

Dr. Dyott believed in the virtues of advertising, and the following setting forth his wares is taken from *The United States Gazette and True American,* for January 2, 1833:

"The Subscriber respectfully informs his friends and the public, that

*Figure 219, page 365.*

his glass factories at Kensington are now in full operation." They made not only window glass but the following hollow wares:

"Apothecaries' Vials from one half to eight oz., Patent Medicine bottles, Mustard, Cayenne Pepper, Olives, Anchovies, Sweet Oil, Seltzer, and Cologne Water bottles, Scotch, Rappee and Maccabow Snuff do. Confectionery and Apothecaries' Show do. Pickling and Preserving Jars; Pint, Quart, Half Gallon, Gallon and two Gallon Bottles; Quarts, Half Gallon and Two Gallon Demijohns, Oil, Vitriol and Aqua Fortis Glass Stopper Bottles; Druggists' wide and narrow mouth packing do, from Half Pint up to Two Gallons; American Eagle, Ship, Franklin, Agricultural and Masonic Pocket Flasks, etc.

"T. W. DYOTT."

Dyott was a most persistent advertiser, agreed to help out country druggists, and sell them goods, taking produce in exchange. He advertised for broken bottles, particularly "broken Porter bottles."

ELLENVILLE, N. Y. Ulster County. 1848. Glass-works established by members of the West Willington Glass Co.

EMMET, FISHER & FLOWERS. East Cambridge, Mass. 1815. These men were South Boston glass-workers and opened a furnace in East Cambridge in 1815. Two years later this was sold at auction and bought by the New England Glass Co. See *New England Glass Co.*

EXCELSIOR CO. Martin's Ferry, Va. 1860?

FARMER'S GLASS CO. Clarksburg, Mass. Incorporated, 1814.

FISLERVILLE, N. J. Works established in 1850 by Jacob Fisler and Benjamin Beckett. In 1851 Beckett withdrew, and Edward Bacon took his place, the firm becoming Fisler and Bacon. The works were sold to John M. Moore in 1857, and Moore Bros. Glass Co. stands on the original site of the Fisler and Beckett Co. The name of the town became Clayton in 1867.

FORT PITT WORKS. Pittsburgh. Established by Curling and Price, 1830.

GAINES, THOMAS. An Englishman working in a South Boston window glass factory induced the Boston Window Glass Co. to put in a six-pot furnace.

GILLILAND. The Gilliland family seems to have been in the glass business for several generations, as agents at least before they became producers. In 1760, James Gilliland, dealer in earthenware, delft and glass in Wall Street, New York, advertised the following articles on sale in his shop: "Enameled and cabbage teapots, cut and ground glass decanters, tumblers, punch and wine glasses." (Interior of ancient glass-works, Figure 220.) About 1820 some workers from the New England Glass Works built a factory which was run under the firm name of Fisher and Gilliland. Plain decanters by them are still in use. In 1823 John

*Figure 220, page 366.*

L. Gilliland built a glass factory called the South Ferry Factory, and though successful at first, it failed in 1854.

GILLILAND'S BROOKLYN GLASS WORKS. Established 1830. The following advertisement appears in Poulson's *American Daily Advertiser* for January 1, 1830: "John L. Gilliland and Co.'s Plain, Moulded and Pressed Glass, and Joseph Baggott's Cut Glass, have been removed from No. 23 Dock St. to 3 Minor St." That competition raged keenly, the following extract from a long advertisement in the next issue of Poulson's *Advertiser* plainly shows:

"John Southan, 23 Dock St., has been the agent for Gilliland and Baggott's glass. But they removed it, and he advertises that he is still able to supply every description of Glass, both Plain and Cut. That he has made connection with the Union Glass Works of Kensington, and assures the trade he will not be undersold. Though he is perfectly willing that his glass shall be removed by the favor of his customers, he does not intend his warehouse shall."

GERMANTOWN (QUINCY), MASS. Had one glass-house recorded in 1750-60.

GLASSBORO, N. J. Stanger Bros. erected a glass-works in Gloucester County, New Jersey, in 1775, which later received the name of Glassboro. Rink and Stanger built new works on the same site in 1813, and in 1837 Thomas H. Whitney purchased the business and in 1840 took his brother Samuel A. Whitney into business with him, under the firm name of Whitney Bros. In 1887 a company was formed under the title of Whitney Glass Works. A whiskey bottle in the form of a log-cabin, one of the best known campaign bottles, was made by them in 1840. They also made the Jenny Lind bottles in 1850, globe shaped, with long slender necks; the same type was also made by several other firms.

GLASS HOUSE CO. New York. 1754-1757.

GLASS HOUSE, N. Y. Rensselaer County. This town was in 1805 called Rensselaer Village, and was the seat of an extensive glass factory. In 1806 the company was incorporated, and was discontinued in 1852. In 1813 a force of 100 men were employed.

GUILDERLAND, N. Y. Situated near Albany, N. Y. Opened glass-works in 1786, became the Hamilton Manufacturing Co. in 1797, and closed in 1815. Made both window glass, bottles and flasks, some of the latter with design of Washington. The tribulations of these early glass-makers were excessive. They were constantly asking for Government loans, and in 1793 the Legislature of the State of New York voted a loan of 3,000 pounds to the proprietors for eight years, the first three years without interest. It was proposed in 1796 to build here a town called Hamilton, the glass company and workmen to be exempt from taxes for five years. In 1792 they advertised for a flint glass maker, and added, "As this manufactory must be of great public utility, it is presumed they will receive the greatest encouragement from all American glass dealers."

**HAMMONTON, N. J.** In 1820 a glass-works was established by William Coffin. In 1836 the firm became Coffin and Hay, who added bottles and flasks to the window glass department. In 1844 William Coffin died and two of his sons succeeded him, making window glass only. The business was closed about 1858.

**HART & CO., JOHN.** This name is found on a heart-shaped whiskey flask, in amber colour.

**HEMINGRAY GLASS CO.** Cincinnati, Ohio. Established in 1848. They made tableware of all kinds, glass lamps, jars, demijohns, flasks, bottles, etc. The works were at Covington, Ky.

**HEWES, ROBERT.** From Boston, built glass-works at Temple, N. H., in 1779 to 1780. The works were not successful, and operated only a short time. Harvard College is said to own some of their products.

**HOARE, BURNS & DAILY.** In 1854 moved first to the South Ferry Works, Brooklyn, then to Greenpoint, and finally in 1873 to Corning, N. Y.

**HUFFSEY, SAMUEL.** A glass-blower in Philadelphia in 1850, and owner of a glass-works in Camden, N. J., at the same period. Made bottles with the Kossuth and Jenny Lind designs and always put his name on them.

**HUNNEWELL & GORE.** Chelmsford, Mass. Had a glass-works from 1802· 1827. It became the Chelmsford Glass Works in 1829. Moved to Suncook, N. H., in 1839; closed, 1850.

**KENSINGTON GLASS WORKS.** See *Dyottville*. (See Figure 221, made 1835.)

**KENSINGTON, PA.** In 1820 workmen from New England started a glass-works here, but they quarrelled among themselves and the business failed.

**KEENE, N. H.** In 1814, by Act of Legislature, the New Hampshire Glass Factory was incorporated. Closed 1850.

**KEENE, N. H.** 1815, the Marlboro Street Factory was built to make flint glass bottles and decanters. Closed about 1842.

**LANCASTER GLASS WORKS.** Lancaster, N. Y. Made bottles; one so marked is a bluish aquamarine with basket design.

**LA BELLE COMPANY.** Bridgeport, Ohio. About 1879.

**LEE, MASS.** Glasshouse. One of the grants of land which were set off to form the town of Lee was called Glasshouse. The grant was made in 1754 to John Franklin and his associates. In 1754 a further grant was made to encourage the making of "potash, cider, glass and cloth." The venture is said to have been "pecuniarily unsuccessful."

**LENOX FURNACE.** Lenox, Mass. In 1853 the Lenox Iron Co. built a glass-works near their iron furnace at Lenox. After a short run the glass-

*Figure 221, page 368.*

works were burned, and immediately rebuilt, and leased to James N. Richmond, of Cheshire, Mass., in 1855. He kept them but a year, and then the Iron Company ran them successfully, making rough plate till 1862, when they were again burned. They were rebuilt, and have passed through many hands and under many names.

LOUISVILLE, KY., GLASS WORKS. This lettering is found on a whiskey flask, amber, with design of American eagle. The company was organised by Capt. J. B. Ford in 1875.

LYNDEBORO, N. H. See *South Lyndeboro*.

MARRETT, T. A. Established 1849. Manufacturer and glass cutter at 212 Canal Street, New York.

MARTIN'S FERRY, VA. Excelsior Co. 1860.

MARYLAND GLASS WORKS. 1850. Founded by John Lee Chapman, at Lancaster and Caroline streets, Baltimore, Md.

MILFORD, N. J. 1800.

MILLVILLE, N. J. 1822. In 1880 there were four "green hollow ware and six white glass furnaces, run by Whitall, Tatum, and Co."

MORRIS, ROBERT AND JOHN NICHOLSON. Erected a glass-house at the Falls of the Schuykill, Pa., in 1780-1786.

McCULLY, WILLIAM. Pennsylvania, 1828. Operated the Sligo Works.

NEW ALBANY, IND. 1869. Works were founded by Capt. J. B. Ford, and operated by W. C. De Pauw, after 1872.

NEW ALBANY, PA. 1831. Window glass house.

NEW BEDFORD, MASS. In 1861 glass-works were started here, but were not particularly successful, and were sold in 1869 to W. L. Libby, who reopened the works under the name of "Mt. Washington Glass Works," and built a large addition to the works in 1880.

NEW BRITAIN, N. J. Isabella Glass Works, 1840. Bottles and flasks.

NEW ENGLAND GLASS CO. East Cambridge, Mass., 1817. These works started with a six-pot furnace, forty hands employed. In 1818, Bishop in "American Manufactures," says of this company: "Two flint glass furnaces and 24 glass-cutting mills operated by steam, a red lead furnace capable of making two tons of red lead a week, enabled them to produce every variety of fine, plain, mould and richest cut-glass, as Grecian lamps, chandeliers for churches, vases, antique and transparent lamps, etc., for domestic supply and exportation to the West Indies and South America. Virginia coal, New Orleans lead and Delaware sand and other native materials were used."

The first lead furnace in the United States is believed to be the one built by Deming Jarves of the N. E. Glass Co. in 1818 for the manufacture of lead for glass. It was a success.

In 1823 many beautiful glass vessels of various kinds were made and sent into Boston. Mr. Jarves states that in 1852 five hundred hands were employed. In 1878 the works were leased to W. L. Libby and nine years later his son moved them to Toledo, Ohio.

NEW GENEVA, PA. Glass-works built by Albert Gallatin in 1797. Moved in 1809 to the Monongahela River, 90 miles south of Pittsburgh. These works were operated by Nicholson and Co. in 1814, and are recorded as being at work as late as 1832. The firm name was Gallatin and Co.

NEW LONDON, CONN. About 1860 a glass-works was established here, known as the Thames Glass Works. It operated only a short time. One bottle was made, an eagle design; reverse, anchor and scroll with the words "New London Glass Works."

NEW WINDSOR, N. Y. Orange County. 1753-1785.

NEW YORK CITY. Had two glass-works in 1732. (Tenth Census Report.)

NEW YORK GLASS HOUSE CO. This company was allowed by the Common Council of New York through the efforts of Matthew Earnest, in 1757, to construct a dock on city land for the use of the company, rent of one pepper-corn being demanded for the privilege. Previous to this they had used a dock for which the annual payment was no doubt considerably more. The following advertisement appeared for six insertions in the *New York Gazette or Weekly Post Boy,* for October and November, 1754:

"Notice is hereby given. That there is to be sold by Thomas Lepper, Storekeeper to the Glass House Company, living at their store on the late Sir Peter Warren's dock at the North River near Mr. Peter Mesier's, all sorts of bottles from one Qt. to three Gallons and upwards as also a variety of other Glass Ware too tedious to mention, all at reasonable rates; and all Gentlemen that wants Bottles of any size with their names on them, or any Chymical Glasses, or any other sort of Glass Ware, may by applying to said Lepper, have them made with all expedition. N. B. Said Lepper gives ready money for ashes and old window glass."

Thomas Lepper acted merely as agent for the Glass House goods, his business being that of keeper of a Gentleman's Ordinary at the Sign of the Duke of Cumberland.

In 1758 an advertisement in the *New York Mercury* reads: "This is to inform the Publick that the new erected Glass House at Newfoundland within four miles of this City, is now at work, and that any Gentlemen may be supplied with Bottles, Flasks of any sort of Glass agreeable to directions. N. B. Any person that has Oak Wood to dispose of, by bringing to the above mentioned place, will receive the New York Price upon Delivery, by

Matthew Earnest."

Ten years later the proprietor of the Glass House is spoken of as a bankrupt in a report by Gov. Moore of New York to The Lords of Trade and Plantations. The reason given was, "he was deserted by his servants whom he had imported at great expense."

According to the Census New York State had thirteen glass factories in 1835.

O'HARA GLASS WORKS. Pittsburgh, Pa. "The triumphs of pressed glass came from Pittsburgh. James B. Lyon & Co., of the O'Hara Glass Works, made for many years pressed glass only, and in 1867 made an exhibit at the Paris Exposition and took first prize for fine pressed glassware."

ONEIDA GLASS & IRON MANUFACTURING CO. They began operations at Taberg, Oneida County, N. Y., in 1809.

PERRYOPOLIS, PA. Flint glass house, 1831.

PHILADELPHIA, PA. Glass worker named John Tittery, said to have arrived in 1683. There was one glass-house in the city in 1810, two in Philadelphia Co. and one each in Wayne and Gyconing counties.

PITKIN GLASS WORKS. Manchester, Conn. 1783-1830.

PITTSBURGH, PA. 1795. There were five glass factories in Pittsburgh, in 1813, eight in 1826, thirty-three in 1857, nine of these being flint glass houses, and twenty-four being window, green and black glass. In Cramer's Almanac for 1803 it is mentioned that "jars, decanters, tumblers and blue glass," are made in Pittsburgh. See Figure 222.

PITTSBURG CUT GLASS CO. 1809. "From 1823 to 1827 when there were only a few glass-houses in Pittsburg, the ware was loaded in flats and take down the river, usually accompanied by one of the proprietors of the factory and traded for rags, beeswax, produce and whatever could be turned into money."

PORCELAIN & GLASS MANUFACTURING CO. This was established at East Cambridge, Mass., about 1787, the place then being known as Craigie's Point. In 1817 this plant was sold at auction, and bought by a new company called the New England Glass Co. In 1853 there were five furnaces with ten pots of 2,000 lbs. each and 500 hands. They moved to Ohio in the 80's. They made both flint and coloured glass. See *New England Glass Co.*

QUINCY, MASS. Glass House from 1750-1760. Appleton's Cyclopaedia gives the date as 1750 and says the works were probably built by Germans, and that only black glass of poor quality was made.

RAVENNA GLASS CO. Made bottles.

REDFORD. On the Saranac River, in Clinton County, N. Y. Had in 1832 a large manufactory of crown glass, which was erected by John S. Foster. This was carried on with more or less success till 1852 when

*Figure 222, page 367.*

it was finally abandoned. In 1833 Foster went to Redwood, Jefferson County, N. Y., and established a glass-works devoted to the manufacture of cylinder glass. In 1860 a stock company was formed, and manufacture continued under the name of the Redwood Manufacturing Co.

ROCKVILLE, PA. A glass-works was started here about 1815; window glass.

ROBINSON & ENSELL. Pittsburgh, Pa. Started flint glass-works in 1807. Sold in 1808 to Bakewell and Page, which later became Bakewell, Pears and Co. It was Trevor and Ensell, 1813-14. At one time the firm name was Robinson and Son. They were the first makers of "white glass."

SAMUELS, A. R. Philadelphia, Pa. 1855. Made two designs of bottles with Masonic emblems. Both bear his initials.

SALEM, MASS. Glass-house built in 1639 by Ananias Concklin, Obadiah Holmes and Lawrence Southwick. The next year John Concklin was allotted land also for the encouragement of the enterprise. In Dec., 1641, the town of Salem loaned the proprietors £30, the men to repay it "if the work succeeded and they were able to." In 1661, in the Colonial Records, the place is mentioned as "Glass House Field."

SARATOGA COUNTY, N. Y. Is mentioned as having a glass-works at Mt. Pleasant in 1801.

SANDWICH, MASS. See page 338.

SCHUYLKILL GLASS WORKS. Mentioned as "two miles from Philadelphia"; made glass in 1806-07, and a year later in addition to some flint glass made both green and white half gallon, quart and pocket bottles. In 1810 Philip Jones and Co. owned the works. They were closed about 1823.

SCHWENKSVILLE, PA. On Perkiomen Creek, Pa. Had at one time a glass-house founded by a member of the Pennypacker family.

SENECA GLASS CO. Morgantown, West Virginia. Made souvenir tumblers with patriotic designs in 1896.

SHEPARD & CO. Zanesville, Ohio. Made bottles, one design shows American eagle with letters "S. & Co." Amber.

SHEETS & DUFFY. Pennsylvania. Made bottles in clear glass with design of sheaf of wheat. See *Dyottville*.

SMEEDES, JAN. He was the first glass-maker on the Island of Manhattan. "Glass-maker's Street," now South William, was named so on account of the importance of his shop.

SOUTH LYNDEBOROUGH, N. H. A bottle-works was started here in 1866.

STODDARD, N. H. 1790. "New Granite Glass Co." on deep amber bottle with eagle design.

STOUVENEL, F. 1837. He is the first glass-cutter of whom there is a record. At one time he had a retail shop on Broadway, New York.

SUMNER, JOHN. 1809. Advertised cruets, salts, cheap cut tumblers, dishes, etc. Decanters in English flint. Factory closed in 1820.

TEMPLE, N. H. In an article by Leonard H. Burbank, in *Antiques* for October, 1923, on "Glassmaking in New Hampshire," he gives a very comprehensive study of the efforts of Robert Hewes to start a glass-works at Temple, N. H. Having apparently insufficient funds to start the works himself, he endeavoured to secure a grant from the State of New Hampshire in order to take care of his workmen, thirty-two of them. They were Hessian and Waldecker soldiers who had deserted from the British Army. He also needed help to build his factory. In 1781 the Legislature authorised a lottery with which to raise $2,000 so that Hewes could carry out his project. But the lottery was a failure, and Hewes returned to his home in Boston. His workmen did not fare so well. They were "warned" to leave the town and it is said that sickness carried off a number of them. There were only two firings of glass at Temple, both failures. So it is probable that no specimens exist.

THUM & BITTERS. North Third Street, Philadelphia. Made bottles in 1808.

TREVOR & ENSELL. On the Monongahela, Pa. 1813.

UNION FLINT CO. Established at Kensington, Pa., 1820, by men from the New England Glass Co., of East Cambridge, Mass.

UTICA GLASS WORKS. Established at Utica, N. Y., in 1810 or 1811. They were soon abandoned and never revived.

VERMONT GLASS FACTORY. Salisbury, Vt. 1813.

WASHINGTON, D. C. "Old Glass House" was operated from 1807 to 1851 under different ownerships. The factory was for window glass, as the following advertisement shows, but jars, toys, bottles and pocket flasks were made by the workmen for their own use, and as gifts to the visitors to the factory. "Window Glass of various sizes for sale Wholesale and Retail at the Glass Works in this city. Orders from all parts of the country will be duly attended to by Edwards, Way & Co. *N. B.* Sixteen cents per bushel will be given for clean Oak or Hickory Ashes delivered at the works. Washington City, Nov. 1, 1809." (From the Records of the Columbia Historical Society.)

WATERFORD, N. J. A window glass-works was established here about 1830, or a few years earlier, and bottles and hollow ware were made. The original proprietor was Jonathan Haines, who was succeeded by Porter, Shreve and Co., who continued till 1850, or a little later. The business was sold and was not finally closed till 1880. Made flasks in aquamarine, with eagle design.

WELLSBURG, VA. Had a glass-works here in 1815 for making white, flint, hollow and other glassware. In 1827 very beautiful glass was made here. In 1831 there were two flint glass furnaces at work, but in 1854 they were demolished.

WESTFORD, CONN. Business started by Westford Glass Co. in 1857. Name changed to E. A. Buck and Co. in 1863; closed in 1873.

WEST WILLINGTON, CONN. The Willington Glass Co., 1830-48, was operated by Gilbert Turner and Co. who also owned the works at Coventry, Conn. In 1847 the company was sold to a new concern, and it was carried on till 1872. Hollow ware and bottles, pickle bottles in aquamarine in many sizes were made. Some of the members of this company established another glass-works at Ellenville, N. Y.

WHALLEY, HUNNEWELL, and their associates, with their workmen Plumback and Cooper, in 1787 erected a large factory in Essex Street, Boston, for the purpose of making Crown window glass. Their enterprise was unsuccessful till about 1803 when a German named Lint arrived in this country, and was employed in the factory.

WHEELING, WEST VA. First glass-works here 1821. In 1829 John and Craig Ritchie erected a flint glass-house here. It was a great success. Messrs. Sweeney put in a large flint glass-works in 1835; this was followed by the works built by Plunkett and Miller. This was bought and operated by J. H. Hobbs, Brockunier and Co. See Figure 223.

In 1864 a firm at Wheeling, West Virginia (presumably Plunkett and Miller), brought about a revolution in the manufacture of glass by making a clear, brilliant glass with the aid of bicarbonate of soda and lime, at about one-third of the cost of lead or flint glass.

WHEELING, WEST VA. 1863, Central Glass Works established here.

WHITNEY GLASS WORKS. Glassboro, N. J. See *Glassboro*.

WISTAR, CASPAR. Allowaystown, Salem County, N. J. 1739-1775.

WILLIAMSPORT, PA. Window glass. 1810-1831.

*Figure 223, page 368.*

# INDEX

# INDEX

## A

"Adlerglas," 81
Air twist, 128, 129
Altare, 34, 35
"American Flint Glass," 241
American Glass, 209-382
American glass factories, 369-382
American newspapers, 10
"Annals of Bristol," 153
Antoninus, 4
"Antiques," 219, 179, 318, 347, 349
Artificial pearls, 37, 38, 47, 106
Assyria, 6

## B

Baccarat, 104
Ballarin, 36
Barber, E. A., 275, 284, 351
Barcelona, 85, 95, 96
Bate, Percy, "English Glass," 123, 124, 125, 126, 127, 128, 129
Bavaria, 80
Beads, 48, 49, 50
Belfast, 126, 147, 174, 197
Belgium, 62
Berlin Museum, 32
Beroviero, Angelo, 37
Beverages, 121

Bird knob, 168
Birmingham, 126, 154
"Blazes," 192
Blown glass, 145, 276
Blowpipe, 3
Bohemian Glass, 8, 51-62, 83, 106
Bohemian glass-works, 53, 59, 60
Bonhomme, H. and T., 73
Bontemps, 106
"Boston News Letter," 147
Boston and Sandwich Glass Co., 338, 341, 343-348
Bottles, 180, 203, 211, 214-219, 221, 248, 253-255, 277, 281, 308, 309, 314, 316, 317
Bottles and flasks, 283-288
Briati, Guiseppe, 36, 56
Bristol, 124, 126, 130, 145, 147
Bristol Blue Glass, 156, 157, 167
Bristol Glass, 152-169
Bristol glass-houses, 152, 153, 157
Bristol glass-makers, 168
Bristol Museum, 155, 156
"Bristol tradition," 168, 245
British Museum, 4, 34, 81, 101
Buckingham, Duke of, 109
Buckley, Francis, "English Baluster Stemmed Glasses of XVII and XVIII Centuries," 144

THE END